1000 Tattoos

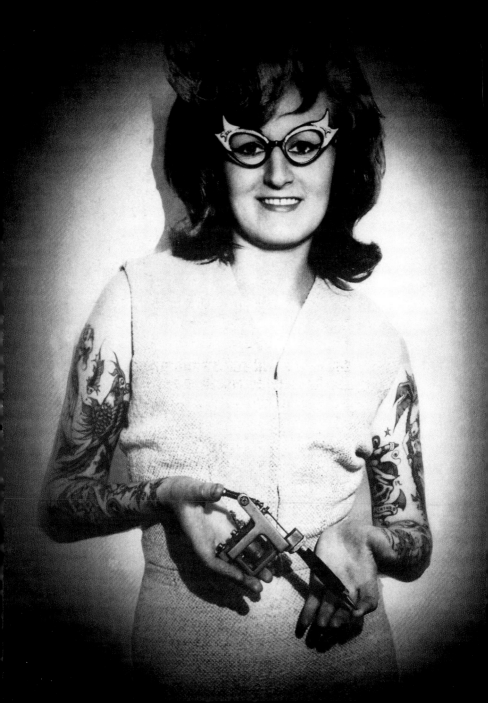

1000 Tattoos

Edited by **HENK SCHIFFMACHER**
BURKHARD RIEMSCHNEIDER

TASCHEN

HONG KONG KÖLN LONDON LOS ANGELES MADRID PARIS TOKYO

Page 2 / Seite 2 / Page 2:
Cindy Ray in her Studio, Ivanhoe, Australia, 1960s

To stay informed about upcoming TASCHEN titles, please request our magazine
at www.taschen.com/magazine or write to TASCHEN, Hohenzollernring 53,
D–50672 Cologne, Germany, contact@taschen.com, Fax: +49-221-254919.
We will be happy to send you a free copy of our magazine which is filled with
information about all of our books.

© 2010 TASCHEN GmbH
Hohenzollernring 53, D–50672 Köln
www.taschen.com

Original edition: © 1996 Benedikt Taschen Verlag GmbH
© 2005 for the illustrations: The Amsterdam Tattoo Museum, Amsterdam
Text: Henk Schiffmacher, Amsterdam
Edited and designed by Burkhard Riemschneider, Cologne
Cover design: Sense/Net, Andy Disl and Birgit Reber, Cologne
Co-editiorial coordination: Anne Sauvadet, Cologne
Copy-editing: Deborah ffoulkes, Yvonne Havertz, Cologne
English translation: Deborah ffoulkes, Cologne
German translation: Marinus Pütz, Amsterdam
French translation: Jean Bertrand, Paris

Printed in China
ISBN 978-3-8365-2622-7

Contents

Inhalt

Sommaire

On the History and Practice of Tattooing

As an art form, the tattoo is as ephemeral as life itself. It disappears along with the person who bears it. Cave paintings, sculptures, and architectural works all have a longer life span and transmit the culture of civilisations that have disappeared. The marks representing the tattoo, pin-pricks in ceramic figures, holes drilled in wood tell stories. Tattoo art also tells a story about art in general. Evidence supplied by these marks is frequently rejected or misunderstood. Until, of course, the existence of tattoo art is suddenly confirmed by the discovery of human remains or mummies, or by the reports of historians and explorers such as Herodotus, Marco Polo and, of course, James Cook.

Tattoos evoke a range of reactions – from interest, astonishment, admiration and reverence to consternation and abhorrence. They are met with open mouths or frowns, their bearers are judged or misjudged, awaking fear or desire. A tattoo always raises questions, whether in the mind of a friend or foe, consciously or unconsciously, whether the person concerned is educated and generous or narrow-minded and short-sighted, approving or disapproving. These questions do not so much concern the technique but rather the meaning of the tattoo, the purpose it serves, and it is the latter, most important aspect of the subject which is usually incorrectly described or not all. There are, admittedly, important ethnographic works on the history of the tattoos of primitive peoples living in distant corners of the globe, but only certain aspects of the world of the tattoo are described, not the phenomenon as a whole. This is, of course, due to its complexity and the fact that tattooing has been and is performed everywhere and at all times for reasons many and varied. Darwin wrote: "There is no nation on earth that does not know this phenomenon."

The technique with which the pigments are brought underneath the skin has not undergone any significant change during the course of history. There are, however, depending on the state of development and degree of inventiveness, great variations in the quality. This is due to the ease of use of the tattooing instruments on the one hand and to aesthetic considerations on the other:

the tattoo should be finely drawn, with lines that are thin, black and even. And then there are the craft aspects: the application of the correct amount of pigment; correct penetration, not too deep, without leaving scars, damaging muscles, rupturing arteries or chipping the bones. Even primitive cultures whose practices involve the piercing of the cheeks – a technique used sometimes with Maori facial tattooing – have developed astonishing tattooing techniques, for example, the Eskimos, or rather, to use the correct term, the Inuit: with the help of a needle, a coloured thread is drawn under the skin and literally stitched into it, one stitch at a time. No attempt is made to depict a realistic image on the skin. The designs are limited to lines, broken or continuous, and crosses, which are combined to form a harmonious whole. In this way, whole surfaces are covered, an arm and both thighs from the knee to the groin, or even the face, which is covered with a pattern of lines.

In the case of other techniques, the skin is divided up into areas by a series of preliminary cuts. These areas are then filled with figures such as lizards or simple forms such as diamonds, circles and stars. Another, less precise technique involves the drawing of lines and curves with a sharp stone. Some peoples, like the Thai, Cambodians and the Burmese, puncture the skin with a long sharp point. This technique, which permits complex tattoos with long rows of dots, spirals or other forms, was used by the peoples of Europe in ancient times and is still employed today by the North American Indians. The technique does not, however, employ black or shaded areas of a larger size. It is, of course, a very good technique for the tattooing of writing, with which we are familiar all over Indochina. There people use the so-called chisel or comb technique: a row of needles, or pieces of ivory or bone sharpened to a point, are fastened to the end of a stick, thus forming a kind of rake. When creating a tattoo, the artist holds the chisel with one hand and hammers on its handle in quick succession with a type of mallet held in the other hand. The points are thereby driven through the skin, which is drawn tight by assistants. In the hands of a professional this is done extremely quickly and efficiently. Large surfaces and long black lines created with a chisel up to five or six centimetres wide are not uncommon, for example on Samoa, where the lines and black areas are flawless and of uniform width. Using small tools filed or honed to a point, simple patterns consisting of delicate lines are placed only a few millimetres apart in exactly the same manner as the moko, the facial tattoo of the Maori of New Zealand.

Another sophisticated manual technique is the Japanese method. With this method, the tattooers use a row of different sticks with needles joined to create a particular pattern. For details they only need up to three needles; thick and thin lines, on the other hand, require more needles, and coloured or black areas require a large number of needles. In the case of the so-called bokashi technique, twenty-seven needles are capable of creating the most beautiful shades of grey in the world, going from black to colourless in one smooth transition. Since the invention of the electric tattooing machine, however, the Japanese manual technique is now used only by experienced tattoo artists and prisoners.

The electric tattooing machine, which was first patented by Samuel Reilly in 1891, has become very popular since that time. There are a great number of suppliers of tattooing accessories and machines, which are mass produced and sold in large quantities. The drive principle, based on an electromagnet and a spring, has remained unchanged since its invention more than a hundred years ago, however. In addition to the hammering devices with vertical movement there are also rotational machines. The latter has a flywheel connected to an electromotor; the rotational movement is transformed into a vertical one via a shaft. The main advantage of this is that it does not make a noise, but apart from that the electromagnetic machine is far superior. Machines based on the rotational principle are only used by amateurs or in prison, where a cassette recorder, an electric razor or an electric toothbrush can be used as a motor. Nevertheless, the results are often astonishingly good.

In both types of machines the needle is mounted on a holder; professionals solder them, amateurs tie, cement or glue them. The needle moves through a channel in a tube-like handle which, depending on the shape of the needle, is pointed or flattened at the end. For professional use, this handle is lathed from surgical steel by a fitter, whereas the amateur, in contrast to this, resorts to ball-point pens, cartridge cases, straws or bent tablespoons, L-shaped holders made of wood, plastic or aluminium, held together with dough, toothpaste, chewing-gum, tar or melted plastic, or tied together with copper wiring or adhesive tape. The pigments are obtained from soot, charred nuts, resin, the ash of incinerated bodies, animals, plants and other organic materials, and bound with alcohol, water, urine, spit, semen, blood or plant juices.

So much for the how – but what about the why? Tattoos can mark the occasion of either a victory or a defeat, can be an expression of joy or sorrow, performed as part of a ceremony or ritual and accompanied by mantras, song and dance. The phase of the moon may determine the time for a tattoo, as may also a particular constellation of the stars, or a season. Some people get themselves tattooed because of certain visions, taboos, oaths or injunctions. The decision to get a tattoo can be a voluntary, sober and well-considered one, but there are also cases of tattoos being forced upon someone or performed in a moment of light-hearted spontaneity. The person may be confused, not responsible for their actions, drunk, mentally disturbed or under the influence of drugs. Sometimes, tattooing can have a traditional religious background and at other times be the result of lust, sadism, torture or superstition. There is an unbelievably wide range of reasons for getting tattooed, many of which are described by Christopher Scott in his interesting and readable tattoo book "Skin deep. Art, Sex, and Symbols"; I will recount some of them here.

The first type of tattoo that Scott discusses is that intended to function as camouflage during the hunt, and that may have developed from body painting. I am not, however, aware of any concrete examples of this. What has been documented, though, are tattoos depicting hunting trophies or a successful hunt. Still others are intended to placate the hunted animal, asking its forgiveness or even its approval. The hunt of cannibalistic peoples or headhunters, where the prey is human, is also shown in tattooed images, for example, the head of decapitated enemies. Among the inhabitants of Borneo there are symbols for children taken prisoner: the capture, kidnapping and enslavement are narrated with great pride in a single chest tattoo. The extent of the catastrophe for the victims is represented by a stylised slendang, a type of shawl for carrying children, positioned on the breast.

Another type of tattoo is performed on religious grounds: people want to ensure a place in heaven and tell God and the world about their devotion by means of the tattoos. Amongst the Naga women it supplies proof that the person concerned is married and allowed to wait for her husband in heaven. Tattoos function here as a kind of passport, as an entrance ticket for the various heavenly spheres. Just how important tattoos were considered in this respect is evinced by the fact that even corpses were tattooed.

In India and Tibet, tattoos provide assistance in getting through difficult periods in life such as, for example, puberty and pregnancy; they also help overcome illness and grief. The latter is a particularly frequent trigger of the desire to subject oneself to the tattooer's needle. The attempt to drown out mental suffering by means of physical pain even leads to mutilation, burn wounds and amputations. (Fingers are crushed or cut off, hair is ripped out, layers of skin scratched off, the incisors are knocked out, and facial burns are induced with hot stones, to name but a few examples.) People commemorate the deceased in this way or honour them by means of a tattooed "in memoriam". On Hawaii, people bear witness to their pain in special mourning tattoos consisting of a row of dots and dashes on the tongue – no painless affair.

In the western world "memento mori" and "in memoriam" tattoos are also common. The memory of a father, mother, brother, sister, loved or admired person is kept alive by means of a tattoo: crosses, roses and banners inscribed with the name of the deceased. Or, to name another alternative, a realistic portrait, or the gravestone with a death's-head. These acts represent an attempt to come to terms with grief, one not necessarily limited to the loss of a person: a loved pet can also be commemorated in this manner.

In the case of pregnancy, puberty or even the mid-life crisis the tattoo plays an altogether different role. Young adolescents take their first steps in the world of the adults and select tattoos which signify their courage, independence and spirit of adventure. They join a group or subculture which they admire and permit their insignia to be engraved in their skin. Their counterparts, victims of the mid-life crisis, fall prey to a youthful recklessness and use their tattoos to prove their independence, rebellion and individuality.

Tattoos on the occasion of pregnancy are less common in the West, since here few pregnant women are willing to expose themselves to the danger of an infection. In primitive cultures, however, people attempt to influence the sex of the unborn child or to ensure its health, to protect it from enchantment or possession by demons.

Another type of tattoo (and one of the best known) is that whose execution forms part of an initiation rite, as practised in many parts of the world. It indicates the beginning of or the transition to another phase of life, from boy to man, from girl to woman, from woman to mother and numerous other significant stages in a life, whether of a religious, social or other character. In the same way as a talisman, the tattoo protects from illnesses, accidents and catastrophes, and brings strength and fertility. This belief is manifested in signs, ornaments, symbols, legends and sagas, saints and heroes. The belief in the efficacy of sacred tattoos also gave rise to the so-called "stop bullet tattoo" which was intended to offer protection against deadly bullets. This tattoo helped the Karens (a minority people) in their long, heroic struggle for independence against the Burmese central army: after receiving the tattoo they became fearless in the face of death. Similar tattoos also played a role in the army of Thailand and that of the Cambodian Khmer Rouge.

For the sake of completeness it should be mentioned that there are also tattoos to protect against lesser dangers, such as dog or snake bites, death by drowning and even car accidents. Those longing for material wealth or the birth of a child also attempt to enlist the help of a tattoo, created during a ritual ceremony by a monk or initiate, who is usually generously compensated for his or her efforts.

Tattoos have also achieved importance as a type of vaccination or for other medicinal purposes; among the Berbers and Samoans, for example, you can get tattooed against rheumatism. Medical tattoos can be found from Egypt to South Africa, employed to combat eye diseases, headaches and the like. The Eskimos and North American Indians covered the skin with signs to protect against disease. The artistic welt "tattoos" of young Nubian girls in Sudan and also common in other African states are not only for decoration but are also a traditional form of vaccination. The creation of small wounds strengthens the immune system, reducing the risk of infection during pregnancy and birth.

Derivatives of this type of protective tattoo are also to be found in the West. American sailors and Marines protect themselves from drowning with a rooster on one foot and a pig on the other. A portrait of Christ on the back protects from whipping, since no slave driver, however brutal he may be, would lash the countenance of the Lord with a whip. Among gypsies and in the Balkans, tattoos offering protection from witches and the evil eye have always been very popular. In the case of the firemen of Edo, present day Tokyo, the motif of the giant water dragon was intended to prevent burns, and Melanesian fishermen protected themselves from sharks by means of dolphin tattoos.

Depending on the environment and the dangers lurking there, there are thousands of ways in which to fight evil and to alleviate one's earthly existence: the appeasement of death's demons, before and after death, assistance in the transition from life to death, from the earth to paradise, from the hut to nirvana. But also the survivors, those left behind, are to be protected from that demon whose name is death.

Tattoos can help one to acquire certain characteristics by celebrating and honouring these very qualities in ancestors and spirits. In this context, tattoos consist primarily of those elements of the national or tribal history which are also of benefit to the bearers, which increase their social status, admonish them to uphold virtue, remind them of their ancestors, of their pride, their tasks in their social environment, the tribe.

Tattoos function as a means of non-verbal communication about deeds of heroism, successful and dangerous hunts, expeditions, migrations, possessions, talent, marital status, courage and strength, inventiveness and perseverance. The lines on the faces of the Inuit telling the tale of a murder are also to be found, for example, among the Mentawai people. The tattooed spirals and lines on the faces of the Maori narrated (to those capable of understanding them) the story of the bearers' lives, their genealogy and their characteristics in an unmistakable manner. It should also be clear that the significance of these are not limited to the earthly sphere but are also intended to function after death, namely, when answering for one's deeds before the judges of the soul.

A more simple reason for a tattoo is the desire to induce a state of fear and terror in the enemy. On many occasions I have tattooed the wildest slogans and the most horrible symbols on people who cannot pull the skin off a custard pudding. Sweating and shaking they fainted at the first drop of blood while I tried to engrave the text they had ordered, texts like "Death before Dishonour", "Born to Fight", "Fuck the World", or pictures of black panthers, attacking eagles or snarling tigers, on their deathly pale and skinny arms. The enemy is, of course, only impressed by powerful symbols: daggers, skulls, black panthers and the like give a message which cannot fail to be understood; "Don't mess about with me!". In the case of physical conflict the tattoo draws attention and distracts opponents, so their concentration on the battle in hand is reduced for a split second – a weakness which can be exploited. This is a principle upon which, for example, the tattoos of the inhabitants of the Marquesas islands are based: large staring eyes on the inside of the arm are intended to put off the opponent for that fraction of a second when the arm is raised to strike. A similar principle is also at work in the moko facial tattoo of the Maori, whereby the untattooed part of the skin alternating with the tattooed parts amplifies the threatening grimaces and facial expressions of the bearer and, in turn, their deterrent effect, so that the opponent flees in fear or begs for mercy.

In the West, such threatening gestures are also part of everyday culture: the rolling up of sleeves and the displaying of tattoos can either deflate any tensions which may be building up or escalate them. Japanese gangsters, so-called yakuzas, take off their kimonos in order to impress their opponent with their body tattoos during the ill-famed card game, hanafuda, which is forbidden by law and played in illegal gambling dens. Mike Tyson is deliberately provocative with his tattoo of the deceased, omniscient chairman Mao Tse-tung (or Mao Zedong), the father of all Chinese, the great swimmer and reputed child molester. Mickey Rourke achieves the same effect with his IRA tattoo. Once I even saw the Ku Klux Klan sign tattooed on a black American GI stationed in Germany: he was trying to out-trick the rednecks in his outfit and keep them off his back. He was given early discharge from the army on full pay because they just did not know what to make of him. In the Russian labour camps, the notorious gulags, where lots of tattooing went on, texts were tattooed from shoulder to shoulder, declaiming: "A Russia without Reds" or "I thank the communist masters for my happy childhood", illustrated with the starving, expressionless head of a child behind a barbed wire fence with watchtower and searchlights. Abdominal tattoos were also common, showing Lenin and Stalin as pigs with swastikas, or nailed to a cross, copulating with another pig, performing fellatio on the devil or puffing at an opium pipe, extreme forms of provocation which could only be removed by treatment with acids or by eliminating their bearer. A tattoo can thus become the most extreme form of protest. It gives people the strength to survive, the ability to assert oneself in the face of daily humiliation.

Another aspect is the tattoo as erotic ornament, one which makes the body more interesting sexually, demanding a response. This is true for leather freaks, sado-masochists, rubber and piercing fetishists, masters and slaves. Or the tattoos appear to be asking one to be gentle, sensitive and tender. There are special tattoos with a specifically erotic message: "lesbians doing the 69", sweet young things showing their bottoms, the Rolling Stones' tongue in the right place, hints as to potency and anatomical superiority, images on the lower abdomen or back which are paramount to an invitation to have sex. Tattoos, therefore, which combine text and image to inform a possible interested party about the sexual preferences of their bearer.

Other tattoos are personal statements concerning love and friendship, about patriotism, or against fitting in with society. A plethora of examples can be given: "Made in England" or "Made in Germany" for the nationalist or even fascist skinhead;

"Mother", "Mom" and "Mamma" demonstrate a love of the family. Perennial favourites are the reminders of amorous adventures: "The sweetest girl I ever kissed was another man's wife, my mother", "Forever Jane", "True love", or, plain and simple, the name of the beloved. Anarchistic and anti-establishment feelings are expressed in the form of symbols considered shocking by most of society, symbols which are frequently associated with murder, war, discrimination, drug use and perversion. Sometimes these are merely a demonstrative pose arising from feelings of revenge, disparagement, or the desire to rebel, but which are not to be taken literally as indicative of the bearer's actual intentions. I once tattooed over a swastika on the hand of a Jewish girl. The symbol, which she had had tattooed in India, went down like a bomb when she got home, something which she had not expected at all! One of the most famous symbols consists of three dots on the hand between the thumb and index finger, and means "Mort aux vaches", roughly translated as "Kill the pigs" or "Fuck the world", and almost guaranteed to be detrimental to your health, should you have the misfortune to be detained at a French police station.

Dates marking important events in a person's life are also commemorated with a tattoo: the wedding day, the date of a loved one's death, a birthday or some other important date or event, place or memory, good or bad. Pilgrims record the goal of their pilgrimage, whether it be Jerusalem, Mecca or Santiago, whether they are Copts, Armenians, Muslims, Christians, Buddhists or Hindus. Sailors who pledge allegiance to neither church nor state decorate themselves with "their" port, commemorate their crossing of the Equator, or when they rounded Cape Horn or the Cape of Good Hope. Soldiers too bear their victories and battles on their skin – the Vietnam veterans and their Saigon immediately springs to mind here. The underlying motive for all these examples is the desire to demonstrate a personal and unmistakable identity.

Or membership of a group is to be demonstrated: one puts one's cards on the table, demonstrates that one belongs to a particular group or wishes to belong to it. For this too there are plenty of examples. In primitive tribes the tribal emblem, the totem, is worn, either a generally known or a secret symbol, such as the magic signs of the Kakean society, a secret society of head-hunters from the island of Seram in the Indonesian archipelago. The welts of the Yoruba people of Nigeria are just as much an expression of membership of a group as are the tattoos of the Hell's Angels and the street gangs in large American cities, and the tattooed symbols of the Chinese triads, not to mention the various signs by which rock 'n roll groups are recognised. They are all pointers, of a more or less direct nature, to show others that one belongs to or wishes to belong to a certain group, world, or life-style.

Circus artistes used to get tattooed as a means of earning a living, a practice which has now become almost obsolete. Only a few isolated instances remain, such as, for example, "Enigma", the puzzle man who works in the Jim Rose Circus Side Show, and who is tattooed from head to toe with a puzzle pattern. The "Great Omi" also known as the "Zebra Man" is the most famous example of whole body tattooing. The travelling tattoo artistes gave spectacular performances in big side shows and freak shows, earning particularly high sums in the USA. Some tattooed ladies were famous, such as Betty Broadbent and La Belle Irene, as were also married couples like Frank and Anni van den Burg. In the States there was even a family in which the son and daughter had the same tattoos as their parents. The high point though was the tattooed cow that pulled a carriage for children on Coney Island.

Another thing altogether is the tattoo with which one can earn money as a one-off affair, along the lines of: "I bet you wouldn't get your face tattooed with a pair of glasses." A Belgian whom I met in Amsterdam in 1975 had won this bet. The token of his stupidity had been removed by a prison doctor but was still to be seen on the pockmarked skin as if it had been chipped out with a chisel.

Although the advertising branch also uses tattoos, no company works with real tattoos of the brand name or the company logo. The "tattoos" are simply painted on the skin and photographed. Or somebody is engaged who already has the tattoo they are looking for. Generally speaking, the tattooing of brand names or logos is not uncommon, especially if it concerns a popular article.

A favourite is, of course, the Harley Davidson, but you also get Jack Daniels, Gauloises, Lucky Strike, Chanel, Durex, Heineken, Nike, Mercedes, Cadillac, Thunderbird, Ferrari, Jaguar and even Rolls Royce. Absolute highlights are Lacoste crocodiles on the chest, and "hip pockets" with the Wrangler logo in exactly the right place. I myself have a Kodachrome film roll in praise of the best slide film in the world, but I have never earned a penny with it.

There are, in addition, tattoos which record medical information, such as, for example, the blood group, which SS soldiers had tattooed on the forearm. This is still common practice in the American and English military, and also in the French and Spanish Foreign Legions. It is, nevertheless, absurd that there are no uniform regulations concerning the part of the body on which the tattoo is to be made, which means that a doctor has to search the whole body of an unconscious patient. I myself once made the suggestion that organ donors should be tattooed with invisible ink on an agreed part so that the doctor can recognise the tattoo immediately using ultraviolet light. It is not often that a person in a fatal accident has their donor identification with them, whereby valuable time is lost. Another point of interest in this context is the use of tattoos to identify parts of the body affected by cancer.

The most unpleasant example is the fascist proposal to mark those infected with HIV with some form of identification. The compulsory tattoo as a form of punishment, the brand-marking of slaves, thieves, rapists and the like is hardly ever used today. A gruesome example in connection with this concerns the Holocaust. Being well informed on Jewish customs, the Nazis knew that tattoos were against Judaic law. The tattoos were not only intended to facilitate the administration of the camps (their role being complementary to that of the cloth symbols sown on clothes: the star of David for Jews, the pink triangle for gays, and other signs for gypsies, communists, etc.) but were also a perverse kind of hobby for the Nazis. The registration number on the jacket was repeated in the skin of children and the elderly, of men and women, contributing to the dehumanisation of the concentration camp inmates, alongside the shaving of heads, the pulling of teeth, and the ritual disinfection of camp clothing.

The registration of a whole people by means of tattoos was common a long time ago in Indochina. Falsification of the tattoos and, by implication, the data they represented, was punished in Thailand during the Chmer period by wiping out whole families. In zoos, laboratories and research institutes tattooing animals is common practice. Dogs, horses, pigs, chicken, rabbits, all types of animals are tattooed for administrative reasons.

Tattooing is also performed on cosmetic grounds – birthmarks are removed, permanent make-up, eye-brows, beauty spots and lipstick are tattooed. I myself have seen a Belgian who had tattoos of chest hair and chin stubble. Scars are covered or dyed in the appropriate skin colour and in the case of mastectomies, the nipple is tattooed back on. Once – believe it or not – I met a white gentleman who wished to become black with the help of tattoos.

The prison tattoo has already been mentioned in connection with the gulags and gangs. The instruction "cut here" together with a dotted line on the throat is used to mock the executioner. Despite the prison ruling forbidding tattoos, which is backed up with heavy disciplinary penalties, there is always a certain amount of tattooing activity in prisons. The tattoo becomes a form of protest against dehumanisation, a rebellion to show that the prisoner has not given up, has not been conquered or broken, proving the spirit in an imprisoned body. The time which has been done is documented on the body and at the same time ridiculed, as, for example, in the Russian prisons with a corresponding number of church spires. The crime, the type of punishment and the pecking order in the camp or prison is also tattooed for all to see on the knuckles. "The Aryan Brotherhood", "White Power", swastikas, "100 % White", "K.K.K." – all prison tattoos of white Americans, white prisoners who have banded together against their black opponents. Other gang tattoos are "mi vida loca" ("my crazy life"), the three dots of the Mexican jail gangs in the USA, the Zigizigi sputnik, the Bahala in the Philippines. In these gangs are comprised of people who have had to decide whose side they are on within the four walls in which they must live, eat, sleep and survive. In Manila in the Philippines, where nearly all prisoners have a gang tattoo, you are thrown straight back in jail if you are found to have one of these tattoos when you are picked up on the street.

The quality of tattoos depends on the stage of economic development and the level of education. A refinement of the culture becomes possible when a people settles in one place; agriculture flourishes, allowing a rich spiritual and mythical world of ideas to come into being, giving rise in their turn to a multiplicity of art forms and cultural expression. Many primitive peoples who do not document their history in written form but instead have an oral tradition, can trace the history of the tribe for many generations, sometimes ninety or a hundred. Body ornamentation also plays a part in the process of detailed transmission as do also wood carvings, paintings, weaving and architecture. The number of times a rope is wound around two beams of a house in order to join them is not left to chance but instead corresponds to, for example, the number of ships with which a people migrated. The triangle tattooed near the small of the back refers, on Samoa, to the flying dog, the bat, and marks the place where the so-called Mongolian spot was found, a blue skin coloration in people of Mongolian descent which is visible in the first six days after birth and then fades. These indications of a person's origins are very important. Nomadic peoples, having the least number of possessions and very few tools, have hardly any tattoos or only very coarse forms. Ethnographic studies have shown us that those peoples who built houses and employed some form of agriculture, who were aware of the past and lived in hierarchic structures, and who were often warlike and feared head-hunters, brought forth the best examples of primitive art. Such peoples tattooed to an extreme degree because their society was a complex one with respect to hierarchical and religious considerations, social status and the need for courage and acts of heroism. Only those were respected who subjected themselves to painful operations such as tattooing, piercing, burning, amputation and fasting without a sound and without showing signs of weakness. "Learn to suffer without complaining" is a tribute to the tattooed person on the chest of Germany's most well-known and long-standing tattoo fan, Theo Vetter from Hamburg. By contrast, a people that has to struggle to survive on a daily basis and that must continually renew its efforts to obtain its food will hardly have the time or inclination for artistic aspirations. The masterpieces of native art all originate from peoples who also practised tattooing: the Bataks, Toradja, Naga, Iban, Kayans, Igorots, Ifugao and Kalinga, the first coming from Indonesia (including the island of Borneo) and the last three from the north of the Philippines. The whole of the art of the Pacific region is that of peoples who are also skilled in the art of tattooing. The Maori of New Zealand, for example, have perfected this art. Tattoos have absolutely nothing to do with barbarism; on the contrary, they bear witness to a highly developed society and culture.

In the Western world tattoos are mainly associated with those belonging to a lower social class – criminals, sailors, whores, soldiers, adventurers, perverts and the like – and at the other end of the scale with the eccentrics of high society, the rich and aristocratic, intellectuals, artists and all those who make life more colourful. Around the turn of the century it was the elite which had tattoos, every dynasty, from the tsar and tsarina to American high society, the Fürstenburgs, the Vanderbilts, from Emperor Wilhelm II to Lady Randolf Churchill. The elite of today is no different: film stars, the kings and queens of rock 'n roll and many artists have tattoos. They are models to be emulated, the vehicles of culture, they determine the trends. Through their image and their behaviour they influence the life, art, fashion, morals, democracy, emancipation, and thinking of whole societies: people such as Mickey Rourke, Sean Connery, Sean Penn, Dennis Hopper, Whoopi Goldberg, Roseanne Barr, Johnny Depp, Drew Barrymore, Julia Roberts, David Bowie, Axel Rose, Lenny Kravitz, the Red Hot Chili Peppers, Pearl Jam, Cypress Hill, Green Day, the Beastie Boys, Nirvana, the Smashing Pumpkins. They all have tattoos, some of which I performed myself. Through video clips, the tattoos, the old and new symbols become hip fashion trends. The Northwest coast pattern for example, tattooed mainly by Dave Shore and John Hullenaar ("The Dutchman"), actually comes from the Native American tribes situated on the Northwest coast, such as the Tlin it, Haida or Kwakiutl. The motif became more widely known through the back tattoo I designed for Anthony Kiedis, the singer of the Red Hot Chili Peppers. There is no better advertising medium than a star in order to make a tattoo popular.

The tattoo is a form of non-verbal communication. It offers quick information. This is just as true for the so-called primitive cultures as it is for the supposedly civilised world. In the West, however, the tattoo indicating membership of a certain subculture requires more prior knowledge for its interpretation than does that indicating membership of a particular tribe. Our world has a dizzying variety of tattoo themes. Everybody, though, recognises immediately the signs of the known subcultures, such as the punks, skinheads or rockers.

It is above all the emblems of the rocker world which are easy to interpret: imposing and "heavy", usually one colour, with lots of skulls and wings, and usually the brand names of motor bikes such as Harley Davidson, abbreviations such as "F.T.W." ("Fuck The World") or a clear and simple "Fuck You" on the fingers. These signs came into being in the sixties and were worn at that time by the American bikers who transformed their love for their machines into a way of life, riding through the USA on long trips like nomads. The first motor bike clubs were a thorn in the flesh to the upholders of public morals, especially those clubs based on the Northwest coast of America, like the Galloping Gooses, the Pagans and the Hell's Angels. After the Hollister affair concerning a case of rape which was never solved, the administrative apparatus of FBI director J. Edgar Hoover, which suspected everything and everybody, found it easy to marginalise motor bike clubs. The bikers did, after all, present their membership openly, proudly bearing the club colours and emblems on their backs. Throwing "undesirables" into jail proved particularly advantageous just before elections. Whoever wanted to become a sheriff, commissioner, mayor, senator, public prosecutor or district attorney ordered spectacular raids to be carried out, never failing to ensure the participation of the media, of course. Astronomically high bail sums were set and those arrested were usually released after the elections, after no charges having been brought against them. When they later made claims for damages, it was the tax payer who had to foot the bill.

In the face of this witch hunt the American Motorcyclist Association decided to exclude shady members. The membership of motorcyclists with tattoos and cut-off jeans jackets was revoked. This small group in any case accounted for only approximately one percent of American motorcyclists. With great amusement they designed their own sew-on emblems for the jackets, symbols which they also wore proudly as a tattoo, as a means of provocation: a "13" for M, the thirteenth letter in the alphabet, referred to marihuana, and slogans such as "Live to Ride, Ride to Live" were common. People joined this group in droves. They published their own magazines describing their views on life, their lifestyle, whereby tattoos played an important part. Manufacturers and suppliers of tattoo equipment scented a lucrative business and started advertising specifically for tattoo machines and the like. The tattoo shops shot up overnight like mushrooms from the ground. There was, however, a lack of information and technical know-how (for instance, how to align and solder the needles), and the use spread of the single needle technique which had originated in the prisons. The majority of the amateurs knew nothing of existing tattoo art and enriched – or rather, impoverished – the tattooing tradition with meaningless motifs such as, for example, castles. Here and there talented tattooers who were eager to learn developed their style, though it remained essentially an amateur one, doomed to disappear. Today there are more professional tattooers and the public is better informed, valuing quality and professional advice. Extremely gifted illustrators successfully found their feet in the field of tattoo art, people like Bob Roberts, Mike Malone, Jack Rudy and Dave Shore. Above all, however, Ed Hardy must be mentioned, who learnt tattooing from the masters of the traditional art – from Zeke Owen, from Sailor Jerry Collins of Honolulu, and later from Horihide Kazuo Oguri of Gifu in Japan. Ed Hardy became one of the greatest tattooers of all time. He enriched the tattoo scene with the so-called tribal tattoo, whose motifs and design had their origins in the traditional tattoos of primitive cultures such as the Iban and Dayak of Borneo. Hardy also became famous as an author – his book "Tattoo Time" has become something of a legend since he wrote it, and "Modern Primitives", which ran to 120,000 examples, paved the way for today's piercing wave.

Most of the photographs in this book are from the archives of the Amsterdam Tattoo Museum.

The museum with library, which was opened in May 1996, is the only one of its kind in the world, documenting the history of the tattoo from a wide-ranging variety of sources. The main nucleus of the exhibits is formed by the Skuse and Kobel collections, which I was fortunate in being able to acquire, as I have also many other photographic collections and bequests during the past twenty years: boxes full of negatives, original prints, copies and, of course, tattoo catalogues of the last fifty years. As a rule, individual prints have a fixed price; Skuse, however, increased the price depending on how much of the genitals was depicted. Most of the photographs in this book were taken by unknown photographers, often the tattooers themselves. I should like to take the opportunity here to thank them and all their models: this book would not have been possible without them.

Henk Schiffmacher

Ethnographic Tattoos

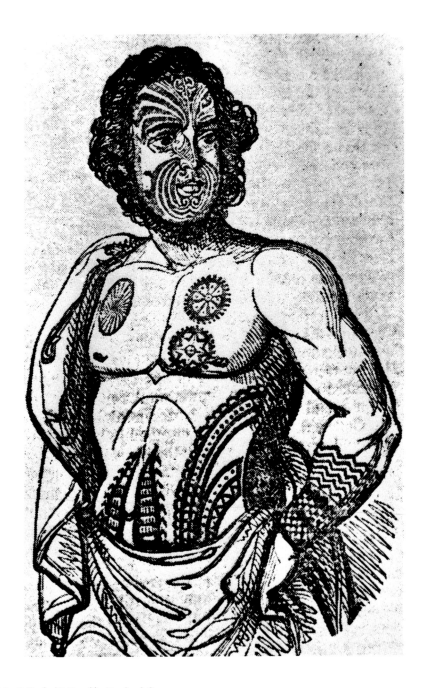

John Rutherford Tattooed by Maoris, 1828

Hula Dancer, Hawaii, 1784

INBOORLING VAN HET MOORDENAARS EILAND.

Native, Murderer's Island

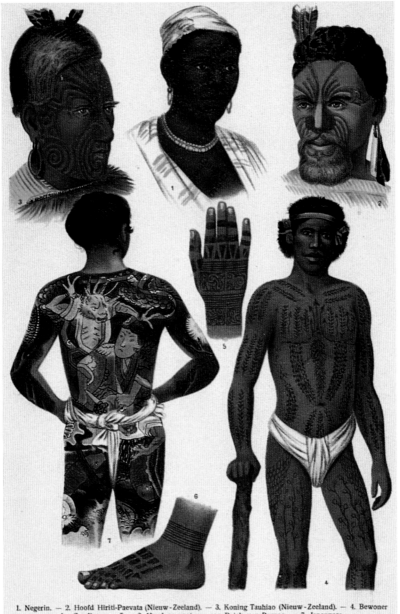

1. Negerin. — 2. Hoofd Hiriti-Paevata (Nieuw-Zeeland). — 3. Koning Tauhiao (Nieuw-Zeeland). — 4. Bewoner der Carolinen. — 5 en 6. Hand en voet van een Dajak van Borneo. — 7. Japannees.

Plate VII.

J. Parkinson del.   R. B. Godfrey Sc.

The Head of a Native of Otaheite, with the Face curiously tataow'd;
And the wry Mouth, or manner of defying their Enemies as practis'd by the People of that, & the Neighbouring Islands.

Natives, Otaheite, 1773

Prince Constantine, Albania, about 1870

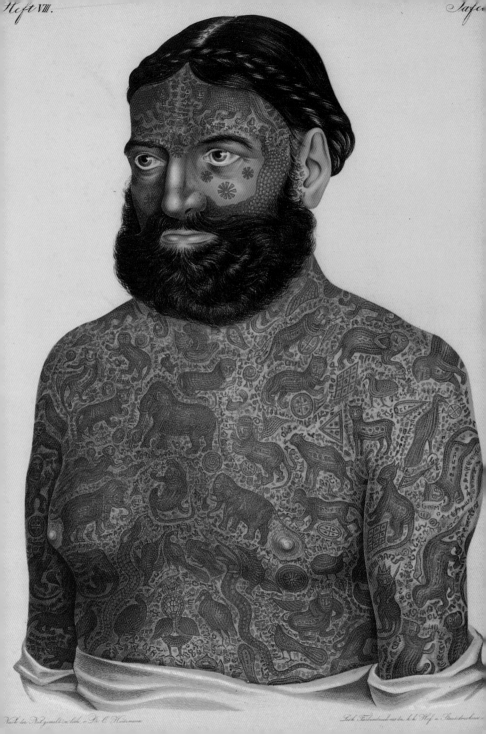

Congolese Girl, about 1900

Sudanese Girl, about 1900

Plate XVI

J. Parkinson del.   J. Chambers Sc.

The Head of a Chief of New Zealand, the face curiously tataow'd, or mark'd, according to their Manner.

Maori, New Zealand, about 1770

Natives, Borneo, about 1900

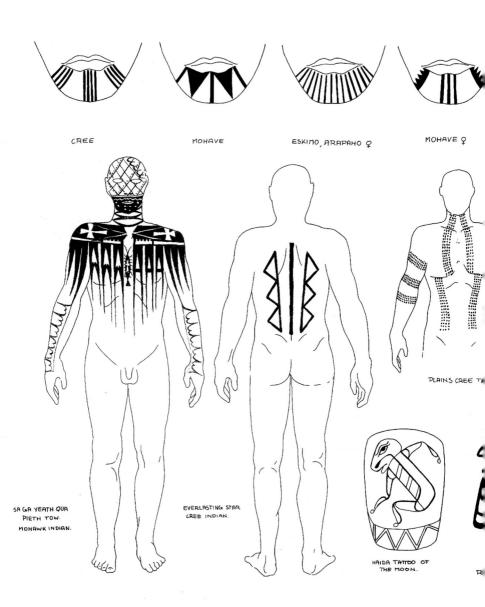

CREE

MOHAVE

ESKIMO, ARAPAHO ♀

MOHAVE ♀

SA GA YEATH QUA
PIETH TOW.
MOHAWK INDIAN.

EVERLASTING STAR
CREE INDIAN.

PLAINS CREE T

HAIDA TATTOO OF
THE MOON.

North American Tattoo Designs by Henk Schiffmacher, Amsterdam, The Netherlands

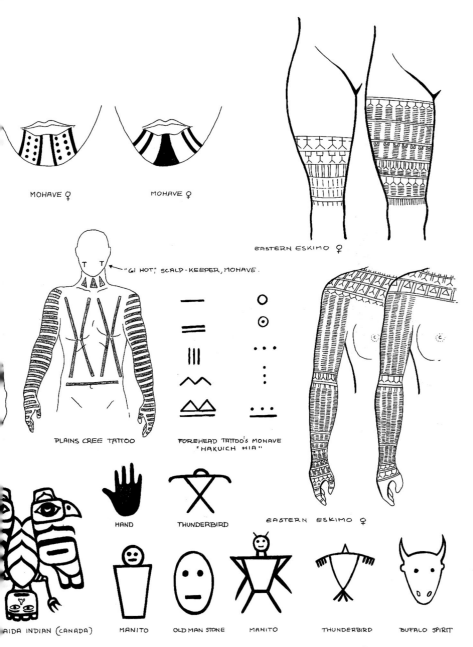

MOHAVE ♀

MOHAVE ♀

EASTERN ESKIMO ♀

"GI HOT", SCALP-KEEPER, MOHAVE.

PLAINS CREE TATTOO

FOREHEAD TATTOO'S MOHAVE
"HAKUICH HIA"

EASTERN ESKIMO ♀

HAND

THUNDERBIRD

AIDA INDIAN (CANADA)

MANITO

OLD MAN STONE

MANITO

THUNDERBIRD

BUFFALO SPIRIT

CREE INDIAN TATTOO'S

Tatoeëeren bij de Nieuw-Zeelanders.

Maori Tattoo Master at Work, New Zealand, 1869

Native, Marquesas Islands, 1843

Maoris, New Zealand, about 1900

Kalinga Chief, Philippines, 1940s

Young Boy, Burma, about 1900

Maoris, New Zealand, about 1900

Maoris, New Zealand, about 1900

Right –

Left Shoulder of a Borneo Warrior

Amazon Indian

Burmese Dragon

Burmese Tattooing Tool.

...rber ...oman's Hand.

Designs Les Sku...

Ethnographic Tattoo Designs by Les Skuse, Bristol, Great Britain, 1950s

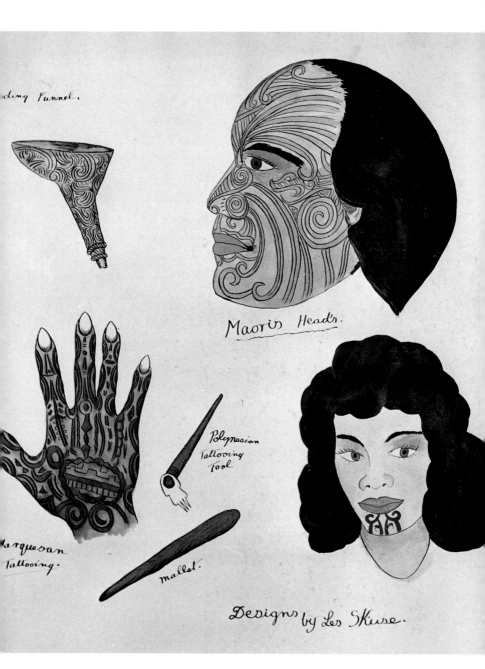

ding Funnel.

Maoris Heads.

Marquesan
Tattooing.

Polynesian
Tattooing
Tool

mallet.

Designs by Les Skuse.

Young Boy, Burma, 1920s

Iban Scout, Borneo, 1960s

Maori, New Zealand, about 1900

Patara Te Tuhi, Maori, New Zealand, about 1900

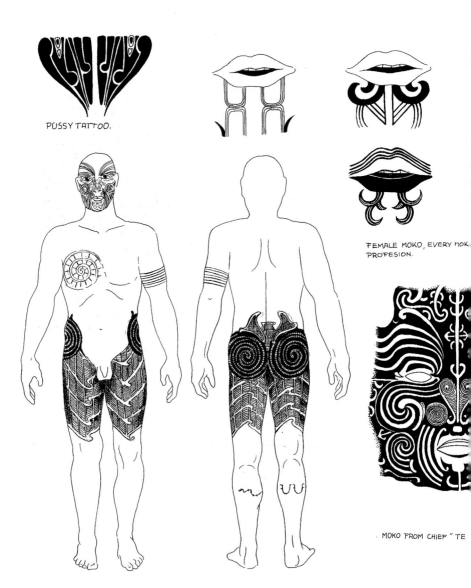

PUSSY TATTOO.

FEMALE MOKO, EVERY MOK
PROFESION.

. MOKO FROM CHIEF " TE

Maori Tattoo Designs

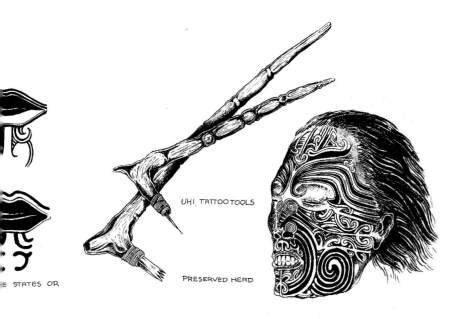

UHI, TATTOO TOOLS

PRESERVED HEAD

STATES OR

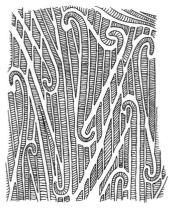

THE DIVISIONS OF THE MALE
MAORI FACE.
① NGAKAIPIKIRAU, RANK
② NGUNGA, POSITION IN LIFE.
③ UIRERE, LINES OF RANK
   BY HAPU.
④ UMA, FIRST OR SECOND
   MARRIAGE
⑤ RAURAU, SIGNATURE
⑥ TAIOHOU, WORK
⑦ WAIRUA, MANA **
⑧ TAITOTO, POSITION
   AT BIRD.
 * RANK,
   SOCIAL STATUS.
** POWER, PRESTIGE AND WORTH
   WAS CENTRAL IN THE WHOLE
   SYSTEM, COMES FROM THE
   GOD'S.

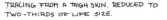

E "

TRACING FROM A THIGH SKIN. REDUCED TO
TWO-THIRDS OF LIFE SIZE.

Maoris, New Zealand, about 1900

Bottom left: King Tawhiao

Tattoo Master Petalo Suluepe, Samoa
Photo: Paul de Bruin, Amsterdam, The Netherlands, 1990

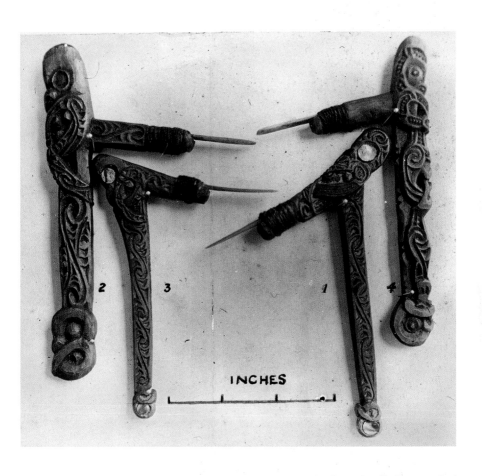

Maori Tattooing Chisels, New Zealand

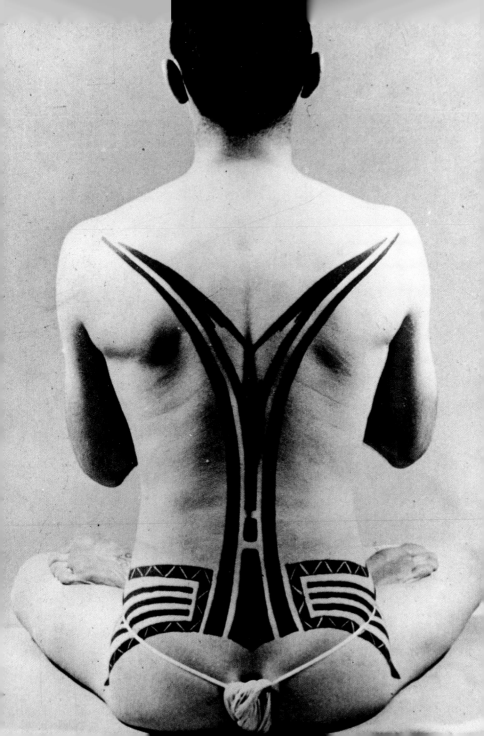

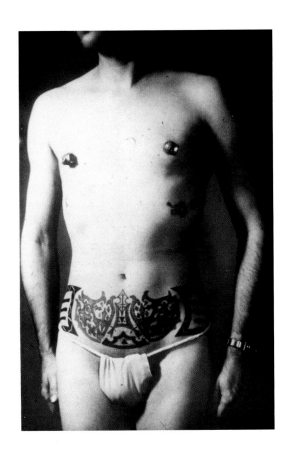

Fakir Mustafar, USA, 1960s

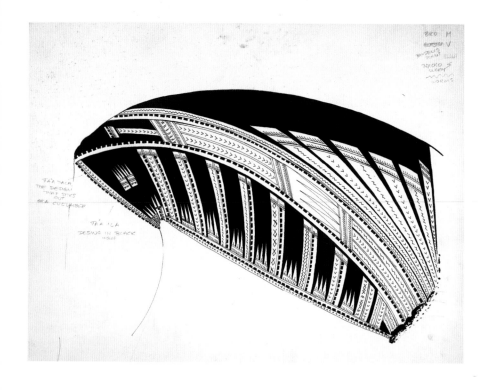

Maori Tattoo Designs by Petalo Suluepe, Samoa

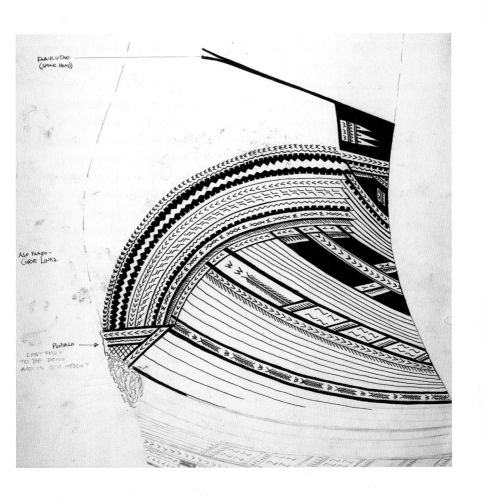

FAAULUTAO·
(SPEAR HEAD)

ASO FAAIFO·
CURVE LINES.

PUNIALO

LAST PART
TO BE DONE
ALSO IS VERY MEDIUM?

Tattoo: Petalo Suluepe, Samoa
Photo: P. Steve

Tattoo: Graham Cavanaugh, Auckland, New Zealand
Photo: Gilles Frenken, 1995

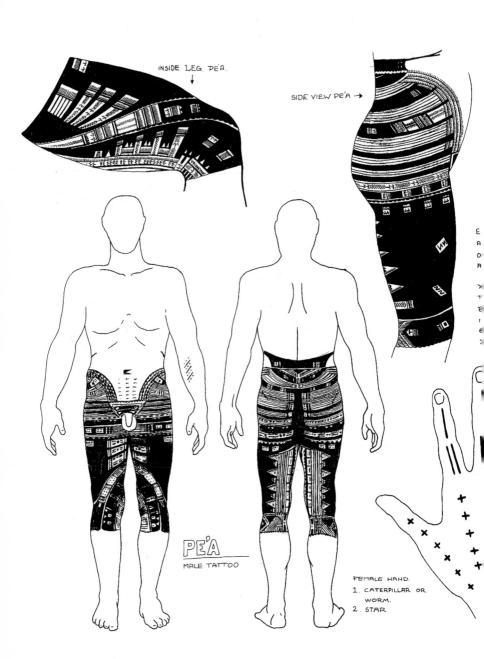

INSIDE LEG PE'A.

SIDE VIEW PE'A →

PE'A
MALE TATTOO

FEMALE HAND.
1. CATERPILLAR OR
   WORM.
2. STAR

Samoan Tattoo Designs

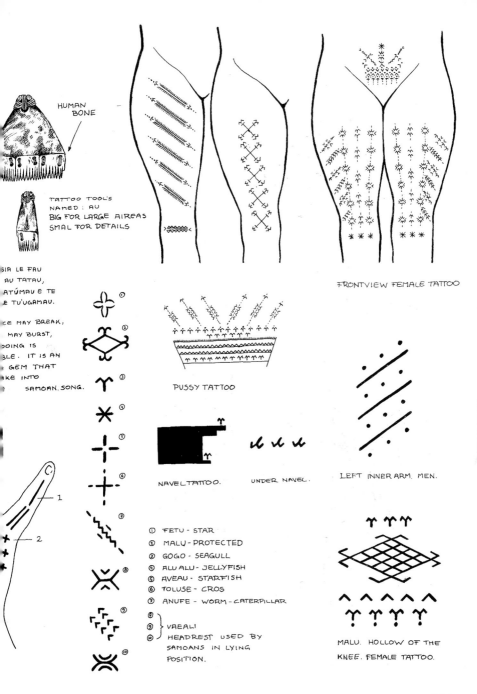

HUMAN BONE

TATTOO TOOLS
NAMED: AU
BIG FOR LARGE AIREAS
SMAL FOR DETAILS

SIA LE FAU
AU TATAU,
ATÚMAU E TE
E TU'UGAMAU.

CE MAY BREAK,
MAY BURST,
DOING IS
BLE. IT IS AN
GEM THAT
KE INTO
SAMOAN. SONG.

FRONTVIEW FEMALE TATTOO

PUSSY TATTOO

① FETU - STAR
② MALU - PROTECTED
③ GOGO - SEAGULL
④ ALU ALU - JELLYFISH
⑤ AVEAU - STARFISH
⑥ TOLUSE - CROS
⑦ ANUFE - WORM - CATERPILLAR
⑧
⑨ } VAEALI
⑩ HEADREST USED BY
SAMOANS IN LYING
POSITION.

NAVEL TATTOO.   UNDER NAVEL.

LEFT INNER ARM, MEN.

MALU. HOLLOW OF THE
KNEE. FEMALE TATTOO.

Tattoo Master Tavita, Moorea, Tahiti
Photo: Gilles Frenken, 1995

Tattoo Master Roal Nuii, Moorea, Tahiti
Photo: Gilles Frenken, 1995

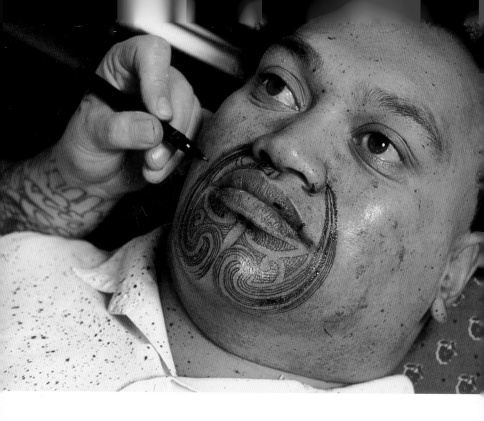

Graham Cavanaugh Tattooing a Moko, Auckland, New Zealand

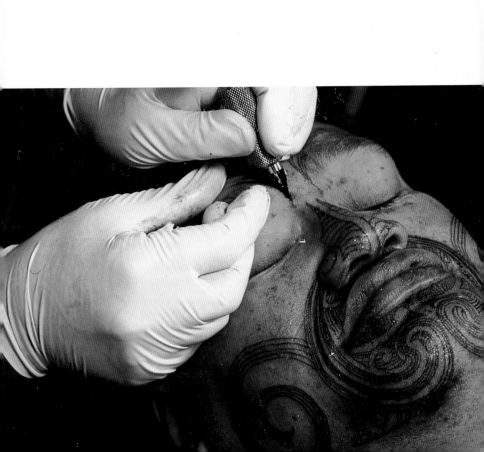

Classical Tattoo Designs

COPR. BY TATOUØR-OLE
NYHAUN - COPENHAGEN
DENMARK
1964 № 725.

LOVE

IL MOR.

Joseph Hartley, Bristol, Great Britain, 1930s

No 188
1935

COPR· BY·TATOUER·
NYHAVN·17·COPENH

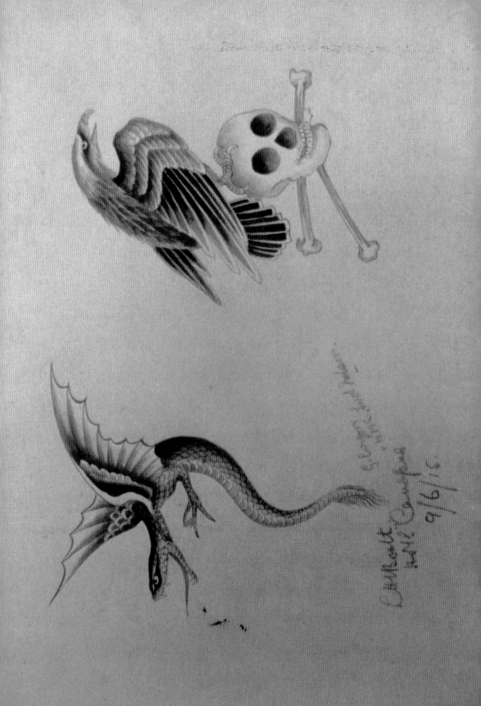

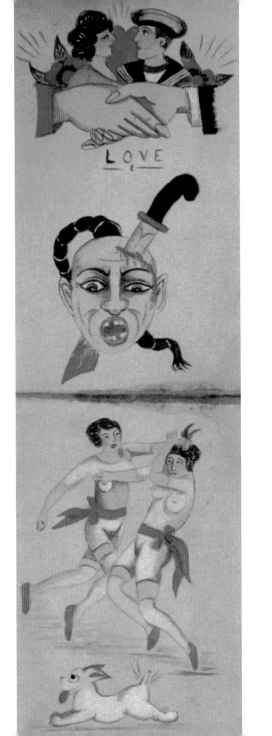

NAME

TRUE

LOVE

NAME

NAME

510

512

TRUE

LOVE

2.30

5—

NAME

576.

519

10

LES. SKUSF

Les Skuse, Bristol, Great Britain, 1950s

Page 104 | 105:
Joseph Hartley, Bristol, Great Britain, 1930s

№ 180/1955

COPR. BY
TATOUOR-O

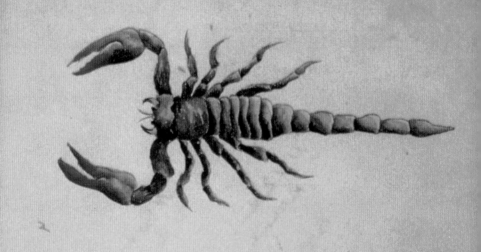

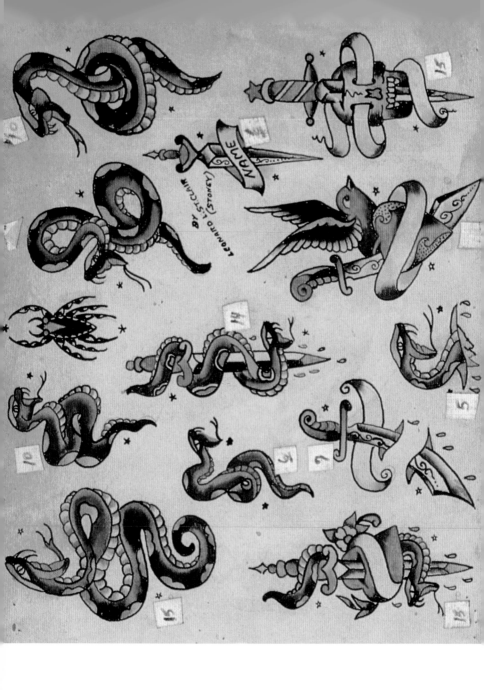

Page 110 | 111:
K. Akamatsu, Japan, 1910s

K. Akamatsu, Japan, 1910s

Joseph Hartley, Bristol, Great Britain, 1930s

21·3·20·4.

21·5·21·6.

22·6·22·7

23·8·23·9.

21·1·19·2.

23·10·21·11.

23-7-22-8.

21-4-20-5.

24-9-23-10.

22-11-22-12

23-12-20.

20-2-20-3.

COPR BY TATOUGR Co

George Burchett, London, Great Britain, 1920s

CK NYHAVN 37.

Tattoo-Jack, Copenhagen, Denmark, 1950s

Page 106 | 107:
Joseph Hartley, Bristol, Great Britain, 1930s

Tattoo-Jack, Copenhagen, Denmark, 1950s

30

35 Kn.

HOME

25 Kn.

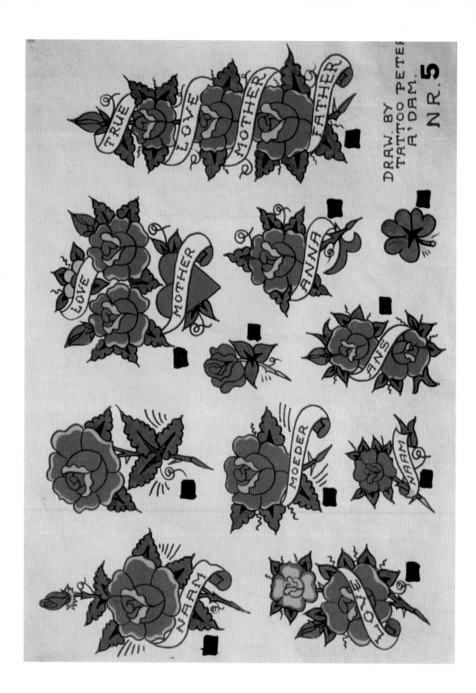

Tattoo Peter, Amsterdam, The Netherlands, 1950s

"Tatovør" Ole Hansen, Copenhagen, Denmark, 1952

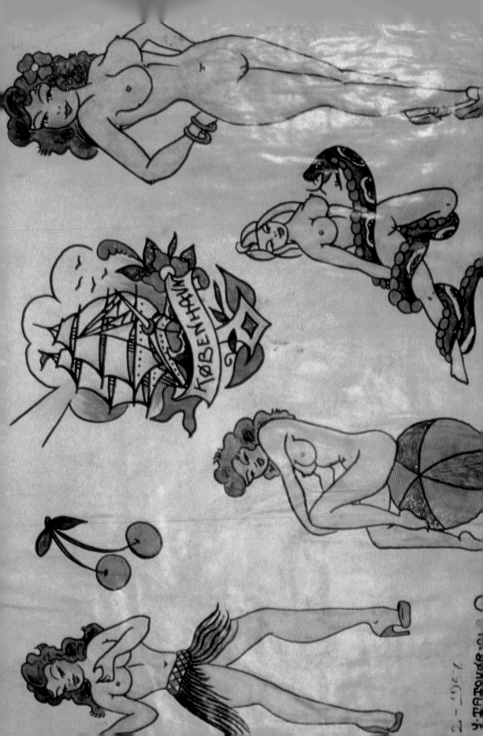

"Tatovør" Ole Hansen, Copenhagen, Denmark, 1957

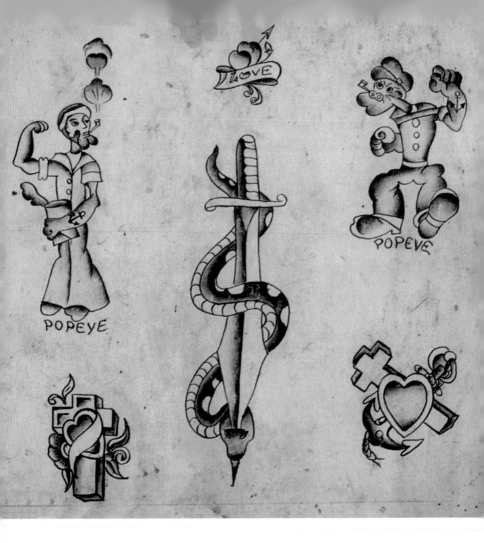

Artist Unknown, Bombay, India, 1950s

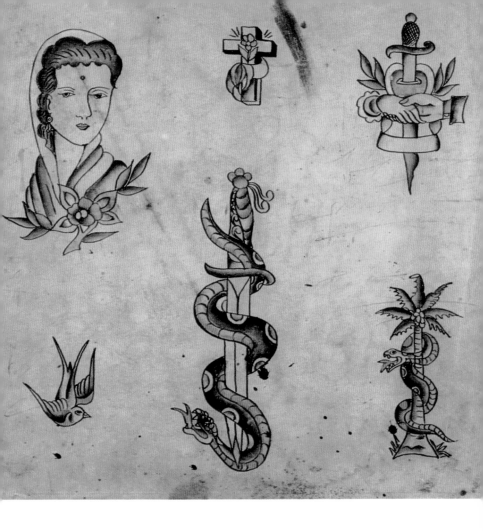

Joseph Hartley, Bristol, Great Britain, 1930s

Tattoo Peter, Amsterdam, The Netherlands, 1950s

NAAM

LOVE

TRUE LOVE

MOEDER

NAAM

NAAM

LOVE

DRAW. BY
TATTOO PETE
A'DAM

NR.4

George Burchett, London, Great Britain, 1920s

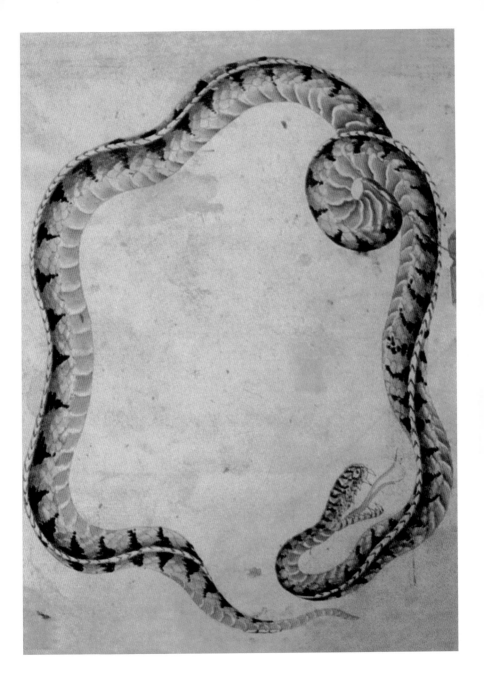

NAME

Joseph Hartley, Bristol, Great Britain, 1930s

Tattoo-Jack, Copenhagen, Denmark, 1951

Geschichte und Technik der Tätowierung

Als Kunstform ist die Tätowierung ebenso vergänglich wie das menschliche Leben. Sie vergeht in der Regel mit ihrem Träger. Die Höhlenmalerei, die Bildhauerei und die Architektur, sie alle haben eine längere Lebensdauer und überliefern die Kultur untergegangener Völker. Die Zeichen der Tätowierung, gestochene Punkte, sind Erzählungen. Die Kunst der Tätowierung erzählt auch von der Kunst. Tattoos bilden eine häufig nicht akzeptierte oder unverstandene Beweislast. Es sei denn, sie werden bestätigt durch teilweise oder völlig erhaltene Mumien und durch Geschichtsschreiber und Entdecker wie Herodot, Marco Polo und natürlich James Cook.

Tätowierungen werden mit Interesse, Erstaunen, Bewunderung, Verehrung, mit offenem Mund, gerunzelter Stirn, Bestürzung und Abscheu betrachtet; man urteilt oder verurteilt, empfindet Angst oder Lust. Eine Tätowierung wirft immer Fragen auf, ob bei Freund oder Feind, egal ob bewußt oder unbewußt, ob bei gebildeten und großzügigen oder engstirnigen und kurzsichtigen Personen, ob beifällig oder abfällig. Sie betreffen weniger die Technik, sondern vielmehr Bedeutung, Sinn und Zweck; diese wesentliche Seite der ganzen Angelegenheit wird meistens falsch oder überhaupt nicht beschrieben. Zwar gibt es bedeutende ethnographische Werke über die Geschichte der Tätowierung bei Urvölkern, die in den entlegensten Ecken des Globus leben. Aber meistens wird nur über Teilaspekte geschrieben und nicht das Phänomen in seiner Gesamtheit erfaßt. Selbstverständlich ist das auch eine Folge der Komplexität des Ganzen und der Tatsache, daß überall und zu allen Zeiten sowie aus den unterschiedlichsten Gründen tätowiert wurde und wird. Darwin schrieb: »Es gibt auf der Erde kein Volk, das dieses Phänomen nicht kennt.«

Die Technik, mit der die Pigmente unter die Haut gebracht werden, hat im Laufe der Geschichte keine grundlegenden Veränderungen erfahren. Wohl aber gibt es je nach Entwicklungsstand und Erfindungsgabe große Unterschiede in der Qualität. Diese hängt einerseits von der Handhabbarkeit der Tätowiergeräte und andererseits von ästhetischen Gesichtspunkten ab: Die Zeichnung soll zierlich, dünn, schwarz und gleichmäßig sein. Dann die handwerklichen Aspekte: gutes Einstechen, nicht zu tief, das richtige Einbringen der Farbstoffe, ohne daß Narben zurückbleiben, Muskeln verletzt, Adern aufgerissen oder Knochen angeritzt werden. Selbst primitive Kulturen, deren Praktiken das Durchstechen von Bauchdecke und Wangen einschließen, haben für Tätowierungen erstaunliche Techniken entwickelt: zum Beispiel die Eskimos oder Inuits, wie sie richtig heißen. Mit einer Nadel wird ein eingefärbter Faden unter der Haut durchgezogen und Stich für Stich quasi eingestickt. Dabei wird nicht versucht, eine Abbildung realistisch auf die Haut zu bringen, sondern man beschränkt sich auf Striche, Kreuze und Linien, die in ihrem Zusammenspiel ein einheitliches Muster bilden. So werden Flächen bedeckt, ein Arm oder beide Schenkel vom Knie bis zur Leiste oder etwa das Gesicht, das mit einem Linienmuster überzogen wird.

Bei anderen Techniken wird mit Schnitten in die Haut eine deutliche Flächeneinteilung vorgegeben. Die Felder werden dann mit Figuren wie Eidechsen oder auch mit Rauten, Zirkeln, Sternen ausgefüllt. Ferner gibt es eine weniger präzise Technik, bei der mit einem scharfen Stein Linien und Kurven gezogen werden. Manche Völker ritzen die Haut mit einem Gegenstand, der eine oder zwei scharfe Spitzen hat, zum Beispiel die Thai, Kambodschaner und Birmaner. Diese Technik, die komplizierte Tätowierungen mit langen Punktreihen, Spiralen oder anderen Formen ermöglicht, sie wurde auch bei den Völkern aus der europäischen Frühgeschichte angewandt und wird heute noch von den nordamerikanischen Indianern praktiziert. Diese Technik eignet sich natürlich sehr gut für die Schrifttätowierung, wie wir sie aus Indochina kennen. Dort bedient man sich auch der sogenannten Beitel- oder Kammtechnik: eine Nadelreihe oder auch spitz zugeschliffene Elfenbein- und Knochenstücke werden am Ende eines Stockes befestigt und bilden so eine Art Harke. Beim Tätowieren hält der Künstler mit einer Hand den Beitel und schlägt mit der anderen Hand den Malet genannten Schlagstock mit hoher Geschwindigkeit auf das Griffende. Dabei werden die Spitzen durch die von Helfern straff gezogene Haut getrieben – beim Fachmann geschieht dies unglaublich schnell und effizient. Hier sehen wir häufig große Flächen und schwarze lange Linien, hergestellt mit den bis zu fünf oder sechs Zentimeter breiten

Beiteln. Auf Samoa findet man einwandfreie und gleichmäßig dicke Linien und schwarze Flächen. Mit kleineren, spitz zugefeilten oder zugeschliffenen Werkzeugen werden einfache Muster aus zierlichen Linien geritzt, im Abstand von wenigen Millimetern, genau wie bei dem Moko, der Gesichtstätowierung der neuseeländischen Maori.

Die weitere, sehr entwickelte Handtechnik – wobei ich das Brennen mit oder ohne Schwarzpulver sowie das Verwenden von Säure, Hochdruck und Glas angesichts der armseligen Resultate übergehe – ist die japanische Methode. Der Tätowierer bedient sich dabei einer Reihe von Stöcken mit Nadeln, um ein bestimmtes Muster zu erzeugen. Für Details braucht er nur bis zu drei Nadeln, für dünne und dicke Linien dagegen mehrere Nadeln und für farbige und schwarze Flächen schließlich eine große Anzahl an Nadeln: Bei der sogenannten Bokashi-Technik bewirken siebenundzwanzig Nadeln die weltweit schönsten Grauabstufungen, von Schwarz hin zu farblos im fließenden Übergang. Allerdings trifft man die japanische Handtechnik seit der Erfindung der elektrischen Tätowiermaschine heute nur noch bei erfahrenen Gefängnistätowierern an.

Die elektrische Tätowiermaschine, die Samuel O'Reilly 1891 als erster patentieren ließ, hat seither immer mehr Verbreitung gefunden. Inzwischen gibt es sehr viele Lieferanten von Tätowierzubehör und -maschinen, die seriell hergestellt und in großen Mengen vertrieben werden. Das Antriebsprinzip mit Elektromagnet und Sprungfeder ist jedoch seit seiner Erfindung vor mehr als hundert Jahren unverändert geblieben. Neben diesen hämmernden, auf- und abschlagenden Geräten gibt es auch rotierende Maschinen mit Schwungrad, das von einem Elektromotor betrieben ist; eine Welle setzt die Drehbewegung in eine Auf- und Abwärtsbewegung um. Ihr Vorteil ist die Geräuschlosigkeit, ansonsten aber ist ihr die elektromagnetisch arbeitende Maschine bei weitem überlegen. Die Rotationstechnik findet man nur bei Amateuren oder in Strafanstalten, wo ein Kassettenrecorder, ein Rasierapparat oder eine elektrische Zahnbürste als Antrieb dienen kann – die Ergebnisse sind dennoch häufig verblüffend.

Bei beiden Maschinen ist die Nadel an einer Halterung befestigt; bei Profis ist sie angelötet, bei Amateuren angebunden, gekittet oder geklebt. Die Nadel bewegt sich durch einen Kanal in einem röhrenartigen Handgriff, der entsprechend der Nadelform nach oben spitz oder abgeflacht zuläuft. Bei den Profis ist dieser Griff von einem Schlosser aus chirurgischem Stahl gedreht, wohingegen die Amateure Kugelschreiber, Patronenhülsen, Strohhalme oder gebogene Eßlöffel, L-förmige Halterungen aus Holz, Plastik oder Aluminium verwenden, die durch Brotteig, Zahnpasta, Kaugummi, oder Teer zusammengehalten werden oder mit Kupferdraht oder Klebeband zusammengeflickt sind. Die Farbstoffe werden aus Ruß, verkohlten Nüssen, Harz, der Asche von verbrannten Körpern, Tieren, Pflanzen und anderen organischen Stoffen gewonnen und mit Alkohol, Wasser, Urin, Spucke, Sperma, Blut oder pflanzlichen Säften gebunden.

Soviel zum Wie – was aber ist mit dem Warum. Anlaß für eine Tätowierung können Trauer oder Freude, Sieg oder Niederlage sein, sie können Bestandteil einer Zeremonie, eines Rituals, das von Mantras, Gesängen und Tänzen begleitet wird, sein. Eine bestimmte Mondphase, ein Sternbild oder eine Jahreszeit können den geeigneten Zeitpunkt für eine Tätowierung bestimmen.

Manche Menschen lassen sich aufgrund bestimmter Visionen, Tabus, Beschwörungen oder Gebote tätowieren. Das Anbringen einer Tätowierung kann eine freiwillige, nüchterne und wohlüberlegte Entscheidung sein, es gibt aber auch die erzwungenen oder unüberlegten Fälle von verwirrten, unzurechnungsfähigen, betrunkenen, geistig gestörten oder unter Drogen stehenden Menschen. Manchmal hat das Tätowieren einen traditionell-religiösen Hintergrund, dann wieder ist es pure Lust oder Ausdruck von Sadismus, Folter oder Aberglaube. Es gibt unglaublich viele Motivationen für das Tätowieren, von denen viele in Christopher Scotts interessantem Tattoo-Buch »Skin deep. Art, Sex, and Symbols« beschrieben werden, auf das hier näher eingegangen werden soll.

Laut Scott dient die erste Art der Tätowierung als Tarnung bei der Jagd, was sich aus der Körperbemalung entwickelt haben könnte. Mir sind jedoch keine konkreten Beispiele hierfür bekannt. Belegt sind allerdings Tätowierungen, die Jagdtrophäen oder die erfolgreiche Jagd zeigen oder dazu dienen, das Wohlwollen und die Verzeihung des Beutetieres zu erlangen. In tätowierten Darstellungen ist die Jagd kannibalischer Völker bezeugt, wie zum Beispiel der Kopf des enthaupteten Feindes. Bei den Einwohnern Borneos gibt es Zeichen für den Fang von Kindern: Jagd, Entführung und Versklavung werden in einer Brusttätowierung erzählt. Die Katastrophe für die Geschädigten wird in dem sogenannten Slengdang deutlich, einem stilisierten Tragetuch für Kinder, das auf die Brust gesetzt wird.

Ein anderes Motiv für Tätowierungen ist religiöser Art: Man will sich einen Platz im Himmel sichern und klärt mit Tätowierungen seinen Gott über die eigene Person auf. So belegt man, daß man verheiratet ist oder aber noch auf den irdischen Geliebten wartet. Tätowierungen dienen hier sozusagen als Reisepaß, als Eintrittskarte für die verschiedenen Himmelsbereiche. Welche Bedeutung die Tätowierung in diesem Zusammenhang hatte, zeigt die Tatsache, daß sogar Leichname noch tätowiert wurden.

In Indien und in Tibet helfen Tätowierungen schwierige Perioden im Leben zu meistern, wie zum Beispiel Pubertät, Schwangerschaft, Krankheit, Trauer. Besonders letztere ist ein häufiger Anlaß für das Stechen einer Tätowierung. Um das geistige Leiden durch einen körperlichen Schmerz zu überwinden, kommt es sogar zu Verstümmelungen, Verbrennungen oder Amputationen (Finger werden zerquetscht oder abgeschnitten, Haare herausgerissen, die Haut aufgekratzt, die Schneidezähne herausgeschlagen, das Gesicht mit heißen Steinen verbrannt). Auf diese Weise gedenkt man der Verstorbenen oder ehrt sie durch ein tätowiertes »in memoriam«. Auf Hawaii bezeugte man seinen Schmerz mit speziellen Trauertätowierungen: eine Reihe von Punkten und Strichen auf der Zunge – keine schmerzlose Angelegenheit.

In der westlichen Welt ist das tätowierte »Memento mori« oder das »in memoriam« ebenfalls bekannt, das an Väter, Mütter, Geschwister oder andere geliebte oder verehrte Personen erinnert, deren Namen in Kreuze, Rosen und Banner eingeschrieben wird. Eine andere Form sind realistische Porträts oder der Grabstein mit Totenköpfen. Es handelt sich dabei um Trauerarbeit, die sich keineswegs nur auf den Verlust eines Menschen beschränkt; auch des geliebten Haustieres wird auf diese Weise gedacht.

Im Fall der Schwangerschaft, der Pubertät oder auch der Midlifecrisis hat die Tätowierung wieder eine ganz andere Bedeutung. Der pubertierende Jugendliche unternimmt die ersten Schritte in die

Welt der Erwachsenen und tätowiert sich Zeichen ein, die Mut, Unabhängigkeit und Abenteuerlust dokumentieren. Er schließt sich einer von ihm bewunderten Gruppe oder Subkultur an, deren Insignien er sich in die Haut stechen läßt. Sein Pendant, das Opfer der Midlife-crisis, verfällt der jugendlichen Unbesonnenheit und beweist mit seiner Tätowierung Unabhängigkeit, Opposition und Individualität.

Tätowierungen bei Schwangerschaften kommen im Westen seltener vor, weil sich kaum eine Schwangere in unseren Breiten der Gefahr einer Infektion aussetzen will. In primitiven Kulturen versucht man indes, mit einem bestimmten Symbol das Geschlecht der noch ungeborenen Frucht zu beeinflussen oder aber sich eines gesunden Kindes zu versichern, das die Tätowierung vor Hexen und Dämonen schützen soll.

Die vielleicht bekannteste Form der Tätowierung ist die als Bestandteil der Initiationsriten, wie sie in vielen Teilen der Welt praktiziert werden. Sie bezeichnet den Anfang oder den Übergang in ein anderes Lebensstadium: vom Jungen zum Mann, vom Mädchen zur Frau, von der Frau zur Mutter und steht für die Vielzahl an religiösen, sozialen und anderen Lebensabschnitten. Genau wie ein Talisman schützt die Tätowierung vor Krankheiten, Unglücksfälle und Katastrophen und verleiht dem Träger Kraft und Fruchtbarkeit. Dieser Glaube an die Wirksamkeit heiliger Tätowierungen manifestiert sich in Zeichen, Ornamenten, Symbolen, Szenen aus Legenden und Sagen, Heiligen- und Heldendarstellungen. Der Glaube an die Wirkung brachte auch das sogenannte »stop-bullet-tattoo« hervor, das Schutz gegen tödliche Kugeln bieten sollte. Es unterstützte das nach Unabhängigkeit strebende Volk der Karen (eine ethnische Minderheit) in seinem langjährigen heldenhaften Kampf gegen die birmanische Zentralarmee. Erst die Tätowierung gab ihnen die Kraft zur Todesverachtung. Ähnliche Tätowierungen spielen auch in der thailändischen Armee sowie bei den kambodschanischen Roten Khmer eine Rolle.

Der Vollständigkeit halber soll erwähnt werden, daß es Tätowierungen auch gegen geringere Gefahren, wie Hunde- oder Schlangenbisse, Tod durch Ertrinken und sogar gegen Autounfälle, gibt. Auch materieller Reichtum oder Kindersegen soll sich mit

Hilfe einer Tätowierung einstellen, die in einer rituellen Zeremonie von einem Mönch oder Eingeweihten, der in der Regel reichlich entlohnt wird, angebracht wird.

Bedeutung erlangte die Tätowierung auch als Impfung oder Medizin: Bei den Berbern und den Völkern Samoas kann man sich beispielsweise gegen Rheuma tätowieren lassen. Von Ägypten bis Südafrika gibt es medizinische Tätowierungen, die häufig gegen Augenkrankheiten, Kopfschmerzen und ähnliches eingesetzt werden. Die Eskimos und nordamerikanischen Indianer versahen die Haut mit Zeichen zum Schutz vor Krankheiten. Die kunstvollen Narbentätowierungen bei den jungen Nubamädchen im Sudan und in anderen Staaten Afrikas sind nicht nur Schmuck, sondern auch eine traditionelle Form der Impfung. Das Anbringen kleiner Wunden kräftigt das Immunsystem, so daß das Infektionsrisiko während der Schwangerschaft und der Geburt sinkt.

In abgewandelter Form findet man derartige Schutztätowierungen auch im Westen. Amerikanische Seeleute oder Marinesoldaten schützen sich mit einem Hahn auf dem einen und einem Schwein auf dem anderen Fuß vor dem Ertrinken. Ein Christusporträt auf dem Rücken schützte vor Geißelung, da kein Schinder, wie brutal er auch sein mochte, das Angesicht des Herrn mit einer Peitsche schlagen würde. Bei den Roma und Sinti und auf dem Balkan sind Tätowierungen zum Schutz vor Hexen und dem bösen Blick immer schon sehr beliebt gewesen. Bei Feuerwehrmännern aus Edo, dem heutigen Tokio, sollte das Motiv des riesigen Wasserdrachen Verbrennungen verhindern, und melanesische Fischer schützten sich mit Delphintätowierungen vor Haien.

Je nach Umgebung und den dort lauernden Gefahren gibt es tausend Möglichkeiten, sich gegen das Böse zu wehren und das irdische Dasein zu erleichtern: die Versöhnung der Todesdämonen, vor und nach dem Tod, Hilfe beim Übergang vom Leben zum Tod, von der Erde ins Paradies, von der Hütte ins Nirwana. Aber auch die Überlebenden, die Zurückgebliebenen, sollen vor dem Dämon, der Tod heißt, beschützt werden.

Tätowierungen können helfen, bestimmte Eigenschaften zu erlangen, indem man genau diese an Vorfahren und Geistern rühmt und verehrt. In diesem Kontext greifen Tätowierungen v.a. die

Elemente der Volks- oder Stammesgeschichte auf, die den gesellschaftlichen Status des Trägers erhöhen, ihn an die Tugenden gemahnen, an die Vorfahren erinnern, an seinen Stolz, die Aufgaben in seinem sozialen Umfeld, dem Stamm.

Tätowierungen fungieren als nichtsprachliche Kommunikation über Heldentaten, erfolgreiche und gefährliche Jagden, Expeditionen, Wanderungen, Besitz, Talent, Ehestand, Mut und Kraft, Erfindungsreichtum und Durchhaltevermögen. Die Linien auf den Eskimogesichtern, die von einen Mord erzählen, findet man beispielsweise auch bei den Mentawai. Die Spiral- und Linientätowierungen auf den Gesichtern der Maori erzählen dem Eingeweihten unmißverständlich die Lebensgeschichte und Eigenschaften des Trägers. Es sollte deutlich geworden sein, daß diese nicht nur irdische Funktion haben, sondern auch nach dem Tod von Bedeutung sind.

Ein viel einfacherer Grund für eine Tätowierung ist die Absicht, den Feind in Angst und Schrecken zu versetzen. Mehrmals schon tätowierte ich die wildesten Botschaften und Schreckenssymbole auf Personen, die noch nicht einmal die Haut eines Puddings abzuziehen wagen. Zitternd und schwitzend fielen sie bei dem ersten Tröpfchen Blut in Ohnmacht, während ich versuchte, den in Auftrag gegebenen Text wie »Death before Dishonour«, »Born to Fight«, »Fuck the World« oder Bilder von schwarzen Panthern, angreifenden Adlern, fauchenden Tigern in ihre leichenblassen, spargeldünnen Arme zu gravieren. Natürlich imponieren dem Feind nur starke Symbole : Dolche, Totenköpfe, schwarze Panther und ähnliches sprechen so eine deutliche Sprache: »Komm mir nicht in die Quere!« Bei handgreiflichen Auseinandersetzungen erregt die Tätowierung Aufmerksamkeit und lenkt den Gegner ab, so daß er sich für einen Moment nicht voll auf die Kampfhandlung konzentriert – eine Schwäche, die ausgenutzt werden kann. Dieses Prinzip liegt beispielsweise den Tätowierungen der Bewohner der Marquesasinseln zugrunde, wo große, starr blickende Augen auf der Innenseite des Armes den Gegner für den Bruchteil einer Sekunde verunsichern sollen. Die Moko-Gesichtstätowierung der Maori dient demselben Zweck: Die untätowierten Hautflächen verstärken im Wechsel mit tätowierten Drohgrimassen die abschreckende Wirkung, so daß der Gegner verängstigt flieht oder den Herausforderer um Gnade bittet.

Im Westen sind solche Drohgebärden ebenfalls Bestandteil der Alltagskultur: Das Aufrollen der Ärmel und das Zeigen der Tätowierungen kann drohende Spannungen auflösen oder eskalieren lassen. Japanische Gangster, sogenannte Yakuzas, legen während des berühmt-berüchtigten Glücksspiels mit Karten, das Hanafuda, das gesetzlich verboten ist und in illegalen Spielhöllen gespielt wird, ihre Kimonos ab, um durch ihre Körpertattoos ihrem Gegner zu imponieren. Mike Tyson fordert die Welt mit seiner Tätowierung des verstorbenen allwissenden Vorsitzenden, des Vaters aller Chinesen, des großen Schwimmers Mao Tse-tung, der – so die Legende – auch Kinder vergewaltigt haben soll. Micky Rourke tut gleiches mit seiner IRA-Tätowierung. Einmal habe ich das Ku-Klux-Klan-Zeichen auf einen in Deutschland stationierten schwarzen amerikanischen GI tätowiert, der sich so die Rednecks mit ihren Provokationen vom Leib halten wollte. Er wurde frühzeitig unter Fortzahlung seines Soldes entlassen, weil man aus ihm nicht schlau wurde. In russischen Gefangenenlagern, den berüchtigten Gulags, wo sehr viel tätowiert wurde, gingen Schriftbänder von Schulter zu Schulter, wie etwa:»Rußland ohne die Roten« oder »Ich danke den Herren Kommunisten für meine glückliche Jugend«, bebildert mit dem ausgehungerten, ausdruckslosen Kopf eines Kindes hinter einem Stacheldrahtzaun mit Wachturm und Suchscheinwerfern. Verbreitet waren auch Bauchtätowierungen, bei denen Lenin oder Stalin als Schweine mit Hakenkreuzen, ans Kreuz genagelt, beim Kopulieren mit einem anderen Schwein, bei der Fellatio mit dem Teufel oder an einer Opiumpfeife saugend dargestellt wurden: extreme Formen der Provokation, die man nur mit Säure entfernen konnte oder durch Eliminieren des Herausforderers. Eine Tätowierung kann so zur äußersten Form des Protestes werden. Sie gibt die Kraft zum Überleben, die Möglichkeit zur Selbstbehauptung angesichts täglicher Erniedrigung.

Eine andere Seite der Tätowierung ist die erotische Verzierung, die den Körper sexuell interessanter macht, die herausfordert. Das gilt für Lederfreaks, Sadomasochisten, Gummi- und Piercingliebhaber, Herren und Sklaven. Oder die Tätowierungen fordern auf, sanft zu sein, gefühlvoll und zärtlich. Es gibt spezielle Tätowierungen mit einer eindeutigen sexuellen Aussage: Lesben in Stellung 69, junge Mädchen, die ihren Hintern zeigen, die Rolling-Stones-Zunge am rechten Fleck, Hinweise auf Potenz und körperliche Überlegenheit, Darstellungen auf dem Unterbauch oder im Kreuz, die einer Einladung zum Geschlechtsakt gleichkommen. Tätowierungen also, die in Schrift und Symbol einen möglichen Interessenten über die sexuellen Vorlieben des Trägers informieren.

Andere Tätowierungen wiederum sind persönliche Statements über Liebe und Freundschaft, über Patriotismus oder gegen Anpassung an die Gesellschaft. Beispiele gibt es zur Genüge: »Made in England« oder »Made in Germany« für den national-bewußten oder faschistischen Skinhead, »Mutter«, »mom« und »mam« zeugen vom Familienbewußtsein. Niemals fehlen Erinnerungen an amouröse Abenteuer: »The sweetest girl I ever kissed was another man's wife«, »Forever Jane«, »true love« oder schlicht und einfach der Name der Geliebten. Anarchie und Outsiderdasein manifestieren sich in gesellschaftlich schockierenden Symbolen, die häufig mit Mord, Krieg, Diskriminierung, Drogengebrauch und Perversion verbunden werden. Manchmal sind sie bloß als eine demonstrative Pose, die Rache, Verachtung und Rebellion ausdrückt, und sind nicht wörtlich für die Absichten des Trägers zu nehmen. Einmal habe ich ein Hakenkreuz von der Hand eines jüdischen Mädchens wegtätowiert. Das Symbol, das sie in Indien hatte anbringen lassen, schlug nach ihrer Rückkehr wie eine Bombe ein, was sie wegen ihrer Jugend überhaupt nicht begreifen konnte! Eines der berühmtesten Zeichen sind die drei Punkte auf der Hand zwischen Daumen und Zeigefinger: »Mort aux vaches« – grob übersetzt: Tod den Bullen, der Polizei, der Justiz, »Fuck the world« – manchmal Grund genug für eine wenig freundliche Behandlung auf einer französischen Polizeiwache.

Ferner dokumentieren Tätowierungen persönliche Ereignisse: Hochzeitstag, Todestag, Geburtstag oder andere wichtige Daten oder Orte, gute oder schlechte Erinnerungen. Pilger lassen das Ziel ihre Pilgerreise registrieren, gleich, ob sie nach Jerusalem, Mekka oder Santiago führte oder ob es sich um Kopten, Armenier, Moslems, Christen, Buddhisten oder Hindus handelt. Seeleute, die weder Kirche noch Gesetz kennen, schmücken sich dagegen mit »ihren« Häfen, mit der Überquerung des Äquators oder mit dem Sieg über das Kap Horn und das Kap der Guten Hoffnung. Soldaten tragen ihre Siege und Schlachten auf der Haut, so z.B. die Vietnamveteranen ihr Saigon. Das grundlegende Motiv für all diese Beispiele ist das Demonstrieren einer persönlichen und unverkennbaren Identität.

Oder es soll die Zugehörigkeit zu einer bestimmten Gruppe zum Ausdruck gebracht werden: Man bekennt Farbe, demonstriert, daß man zu einer bestimmten Gruppe gehört oder dazu gehören will. Auch hierzu gibt es genügend Beispiele. Bei primitiven Stämmen trägt man die Stammesabzeichen, das Totem, ein allgemein bekanntes oder geheimes Zeichen, wie die magischen Zeichen des Kakean-Bundes, eines Geheimbundes von Kopfjägern auf der Insel Ceram im indonesischen Archipel. Die Narbentätowierungen der Joruba in Nigeria bringen genauso die Gruppenzugehörigkeit zum Ausdruck wie die tätowierten Zeichen der chinesischen Triaden, die Tätowierungen der Hells Angels und der Straßenbanden in den amerikanischen Großstädten, aber auch die diversen Erkennungszeichen der Rock'n'Roll-Bands. Alle deuten, mehr oder weniger direkt, darauf hin, daß man sich einer bestimmten Gruppe, einer Welt, einem Lebensgefühl zurechnet oder es zumindest möchte.

Früher ließen sich Zirkusartisten tätowieren, um damit ihren Lebensunterhalt zu verdienen, eine mittlerweile unübliche Praxis. Es gibt nur noch ganz vereinzelte Fälle, wie zum Beispiel »Enigma«, der Puzzlemann der Jim Rose Circus Side Show, der von Kopf bis Fuß mit einem Puzzlemuster tätowiert ist. Der »Great Omi« oder auch der »Zebramann« ist das berühmteste Beispiel für Ganzkörpertätowierung. Die herumreisenden tätowierten Artisten hatten spektakuläre Auftritte bei den großen Side Shows, beim Freak-Zirkus, und verdienten vor allem in den USA sehr gut. Berühmt waren die tätowierten Damen Betty Broadbent, La Belle Irene und auch Ehepaare wie Frank und Anni van den Burg. In den Staaten gab es sogar eine Familie, bei der Sohn und Tochter die gleichen Tätowierungen wie die Eltern trugen. Den Höhepunkt bildete aber die tätowierte Kuh, die auf Coney Island einen Karren für Kinder zog.

Etwas anderes ist die Tätowierung, mit der man einmalig Geld verdienen kann, à la: »Ich wette, daß du dir keine Brille ins Gesicht tätowieren läßt.« Und der Belgier, den ich 1975 in Amsterdam traf, hatte die Wette gewonnen. Der Unsinn war zwar vom Gefängnisarzt entfernt worden, war aber immer noch – wie von einem Meißel herausgeschlagen – auf der pockennarbigen Haut zu sehen.

Auch wenn die Werbebranche heutzutage Tätowierungen einsetzt, gibt es keine Firma, die mit echten Tätowierungen des Markennamens oder des Firmenlogos arbeitet. Die Tätowierung wird einfach auf die Haut gemalt und fotografiert. Oder man engagiert jemanden, der bereits die gewünschte Tätowierung hat. Im Alltag ist das Tätowieren von Markenzeichen oder Logos nicht ungewöhnlich, vor allem wenn es sich um populäre Artikel handelt. Beliebt ist natürlich die Harley Davidson; aber auch Jack Daniels, Gauloises, Lucky Strike, Chanel, Durex, Heineken, Nike, Mercedes, Cadillac, Thunderbird, Ferrari, Jaguar und sogar Rolls-Royce kommen vor. Absolute Highlights sind Lacoste-Krokodile auf der Brust und Gesäßtaschen mit Wrangler-Abzeichen an genau der Stelle, wo sie hingehören. Ich selbst habe eine Kodachrome-Filmrolle als Ode an den weltbesten Diafilm, aber das hat mir nie einen Pfennig eingebracht.

Ferner gibt es Tätowierungen, mit denen medizinische Informationen registriert werden, wie z.B. die Blutgruppe, die sich die SS-Soldaten auf den Unterarm tätowieren ließen. Diese Praxis ist heute noch beim amerikanischen und englischen Militär verbreitet, ebenso wie in der französischen und spanischen Fremdenlegion. Absurd ist allerdings, daß es keine einheitliche Regelungen über die Körperstelle gibt, an der die Tätowierung vorgenommen wird, so daß der Arzt einen ohnmächtigen Patienten am ganzen Körper absuchen muß. Ich selbst habe einmal vorgeschlagen, Organspender mit unsichtbarer Tinte an einer vereinbarten Stelle zu tätowieren, so daß sie der Arzt unter ultraviolettem Licht sofort erkennen kann. Selten hat ein tödlich Verunglückter seinen Spenderausweis bei sich, wodurch wertvolle Zeit verlorengeht. Auch bei Bestrahlungen werden Tätowierungen zur Kennzeichnung krebskranker Körperstellen verwendet.

Das unangenehmste Beispiel ist der faschistische Vorschlag, HIV-Infizierte mit einem Erkennungszeichen zu markieren. Die aufgezwungene Tätowierung als Strafe, als Brandzeichen bei Sklaven, Dieben, Vergewaltigern und ähnliches ist kaum noch gebräuchlich. Ein grausames Beispiel in diesem Zusammenhang ist der Holocaust. Da sie gut über die jüdischen Gebräuche informiert waren, wußten die Nazis, daß Tätowierungen nach Mosaischem Gesetz für Juden verboten waren. Die Tätowierungen dienten nicht nur der Lagerverwaltung, sondern waren auch ein perverser Zeitvertreib der Nazis. Die Wiederholung der auf die Kleidung genähten Symbole (der Davidstern für die Juden, der rosa Winkel für Homosexuelle, weitere Zeichen für Roma und Sinti und Kommunisten) und Registrierungsnummern auf der Haut von Kindern und Greisen, von Männern und Frauen trug zur Dehumanisierung der KZ-Insassen bei, genau wie das Kahlscheren, das Ziehen der Zähne, die Desinfektion der Lagerkleidung.

Die Registrierung eines ganzen Volkes durch Tätowierung war vor langer Zeit in Indochina üblich. Fälschungen der Tätowierungen, also der Daten, wurden in Thailand mit der Ausrottung ganzer Familien bestraft. In Tiergärten, Laboren und Forschungsinstituten ist es nicht unüblich, aus verwaltungstechnischen Gründen Hunde, Pferde, Schweine, Hühner, Kaninchen, alle möglichen Tiere zu tätowieren.

Schließlich sei noch die Tätowierung aus kosmetischen Gründen erwähnt, das Entfernen von Pigmentflecken, die Dauer-Make-up-Tätowierung, Augenbrauen, Schönheitsflecken, Lippenstift. Ich selber habe einen Belgier gesehen, der sich Brusthaar und Bartstoppeln hat tätowieren lassen. Ferner gibt es das Tätowieren eines Warzenhofes bei teilweiser Brustamputation, das Überdecken oder das Einfärben von Narben im passenden Hautton. Einmal unterhielt ich mich mit einem weißen Herrn, der mit Hilfe der Tätowierung Schwarzer werden wollte.

Die Gefängnistätowierung wurde schon im Zusammenhang mit den Gulags und den Gangs erwähnt. Das »cut here« mit einer gestrichelten Linie auf dem Hals ist eine spöttische Gebrauchsanleitung für den Henker. Trotz des in der Regel geltenden Verbots durch die Gefängnisleitung unter Androhung schwerer Disziplinarstrafen wird in den Gefängnissen immer weiter tätowiert. Die Tätowierung wird so zum Protest gegen die Entmenschlichung, zur Rebellion, als Zeichen dafür, nicht aufzugeben, nicht besiegt oder gebrochen zu sein, der Beweis eines freien Geistes in einem gefangenen Körper. Die abgesessene Zeit wird auf dem Körper dokumentiert und zugleich ins Lächerliche gezogen, wie zum Beispiel in den russischen Gefängnissen mit einer entsprechenden Anzahl von Kirchtürmen. Auch das Delikt, die Art der Strafe und die Rangordnung im Lager oder Gefängnis werden deutlich sichtbar auf den Fingerknöcheln angebracht:»The Arian Brotherhood«,»White Power«, Hakenkreuze,»100 % White«,»K.K.K.« sind Gefängnistätowierungen der weißen Amerikaner, die auf das Bündnis der weißen Gefangenen gegen Schwarze. Andere Gangtätowierungen sind»mi vida loca« (»mein verrücktes Leben«), die drei Punkte der Chicanos in den USA, der Zigizi Sputnik, die Bahala – diese Gangs entstehen aus Gruppen, die sich für eine Partei entschieden haben innerhalb der vier Mauern, in denen sie leben, wohnen, essen, schlafen und überleben müssen. Im philippinischen Manila, wo fast alle Gefangenen eine Gang-Tätowierung haben, landet man sofort wieder hinter Gittern , wenn man mit dieser Tätowierung auf der Straße aufgegriffen wird.

Die Qualität der Tätowierung hängt ab vom wirtschaftlichen Entwicklungsstand und dem Bildungsniveau. Eine kulturelle Verfeinerung ist dann möglich, wenn ein Volk an einem Ort seßhaft wird, die Landwirtschaft floriert, so daß eine reiche spirituelle und mythische Gedankenwelt entstehen kann; dann können sich auch vielfältige Kunst- und Kulturformen ausprägen. Bei vielen primitiven Völkern, die keine schriftlich festgehaltene, sondern nur eine mündlich tradierte Geschichte kennen, kann man anhand der Tätowierungen – manchmal bis zu 90 oder 100 Generationen – die Stammesgeschichte zurückverfolgen. Körperverzierungen dienen der genauen Überlieferung, wie auch Holzschnitzereien, Bilder, Webkunst oder Architektur. Die Anzahl der Wicklungen, mit denen zwei Balken eines Hauses zusammengebunden werden, ist nicht dem Zufall überlassen, sondern gibt zum Beispiel die überlieferte Zahl der Schiffe an, mit denen sich ein Volk auf die Reise begab. Das tätowierte Dreieck, das in der Nähe des Kreuzbeines unterhalb des Hosenbundes angebracht ist, verweist auf Samoa auf den fliegenden Hund, die Fledermaus, und kennzeichnet die Stelle, an der sich der sogenannte Mongolenfleck befand, eine blaue Hautverfärbung bei Menschen mongolo-asiatischer Herkunft, der in den ersten sechs Tagen nach der Geburt sichtbar ist und dann verblaßt.

Diese Hinweise auf die Herkunft sind sehr wichtig. Als das Volk mit dem geringsten Besitz und den wenigsten Werkzeugen haben nomadische Völker oft kaum Tätowierungen oder nur in grober Form. Ethnographische Studien haben belegt, daß die Völker, die Häuser gebaut und Landbau betrieben haben, die sich der Vergangenheit bewußt waren, die in hierarchischen Strukturen lebten, die oft kriegerische und gefürchtete Kopfjäger waren, Höhepunkte primitiver Kunst hervorgebracht haben. Solche Völker tätowierten und tätowieren, weil ihr Zusammenleben in bezug auf Hierarchie, Religion, Ansehen sowie auf die Ansprüche an Mut und Heldentum komplex ist. Nur diejenigen wurden respektiert, die sich klaglos und ohne Anzeichen von Schwäche schmerzhaften Operationen unterziehen, wie Tätowierung, Piercing, Verbrennung, Amputation und Fasten. »Lerne zu leiden, ohne zu klagen« steht als Ode an den tätowierten Menschen auf der Brust von Deutschlands bekanntestem Tätowierfan der ersten Stunde, dem Hamburger Theo Vetter. Ein Volk aber, das täglich ums Überleben bangt und mit immer neuer Mühe seine Nahrung sichern muß, wird kaum die Zeit und Muße für künstlerische Ambitionen haben. Die Meisterwerke der Eingeborenenkunst stammen alle von tätowierenden Völkern: Bataker, Toradja, Naga, Iban, Kayan, Igorot, Ifugo und Kalinga, die ersteren aus Indonesien (einschließlich Borneos), die drei letzten aus dem Norden der Philippinen. Die gesamte Kunst des Pazifikraums stammt von Völkern, die auch in der Kunst des Tätowierens bewandert sind. Die Maori in Neuseeland haben diese Kunst bis zur Vollendung entwickelt. Tätowierungen haben rein gar nichts mit Barbarentum zu tun, im Gegenteil, sie bezeugen eine hochentwickelte Gemeinschaft und Kultur!

In der industrialisierten Welt werden mit Tätowierungen zunächst Angehörige von sozial niedrigen Gesellschaftsschichten assoziiert, mit Kriminellen, Seeleuten, Huren, Soldaten, Abenteurern oder Perversen, aber auch mit Ekzentrikern der High Society, Reichen und Angehörigen der Fürstenhäuser, Intellektuellen, Künstlern und allen, die das Leben farbiger machen. Um die Jahrhundertwende war die Elite tätowiert, jedes Fürstenhaus, vom Zaren und der Zarin bis zu den amerikanischen oberen Zehntausend, den Fürstenburgs, Vanderbilts, von Kaiser Wilhelm II. bis zu Lady Churchill. Das

gleiche gilt auch für die heutige Elite: Filmstars, die Kings of
Rock'n'Roll und viele Künstler tragen Tätowierungen. Sie sind
Vorbilder, Kulturträger, Trendsetter. Sie beeinflussen durch ihr
Image und ihr Verhalten das Leben, die Kunst, die Mode, die Moral,
die Demokratie, die Emanzipation, das Denken von ganzen Gesell-
schaften: Menschen wie Mickey Rourke, Sean Connery, Sean Penn,
Dennis Hopper, Whoopi Goldberg, Roseanne Barr, Johnny Depp,
Drew Barrymore, Julia Roberts, David Bowie, Axel Rose, Lenny
Kravitz, die Red Hot Chili Peppers, Pearl Jam, Cypress Hill, Green
Day, die Beastie Boys, Nirvana, die Smashing Pumpkins – sie alle
haben Tätowierungen, einige davon sind von mir. Durch Videoclips
werden die Tätowierungen, die alten und neuen Symbole, zu
hippen Modetrends. Das Northwestcoast-Muster zum Beispiel,
das vor allem von Dave Shore und John Hullenaar»The Dutchman«
tätowiert wird, stammt eigentlich von den an der Nordwestküste
ansässigen indianischen Stämmen, wie den Tlingit, Haida oder
Kwakiutl. Besonders bekannt wurde das Motiv durch das von mir
gestaltete Rückenbild von Anthony Kiedis, Sänger der Red Hot
Chili Peppers. Es gibt keinen besseren Werbeträger als einen
Prominenten, um ein Tattoo populär zu machen.

Die Tätowierung ist eine Form der nichtsprachlichen Kommunikation. Sie bietet schnelle Information. Das gilt sowohl für die
sogenannten »primitiven Kulturen« als auch für die sogenannte
»zivilisierte Welt«. Hier im Westen muß der Betrachter allerdings
meist mehr Vorwissen haben als ein Mitglied einer bestimmten
Stammeskultur. Unsere Welt zeichnet sich durch einen enormen
Variantenreichtum an Tätowierungen aus. Die Zeichen der bekannten
Subkulturen, wie Punks, Skinheads oder Rocker, erkennt jeder allerdings auf Anhieb.

Vor allem die Abzeichen der Rockerwelt sind leicht zu ent-
schlüsseln: imponierend, schwer, meist einfarbig, mit vielen
Schädeln und Flügeln, außerdem die Markenzeichen von Motor-
rädern, wie Harley Davidson, Abkürzungen wie »F.T.W.« (»Fuck the
World«) oder einfach und deutlich ein »Fuck You« auf den Fingern.
Diese Zeichen sind in den Sechzigern entstanden und wurden
damals von den amerikanischen Bikern getragen, die ihre Liebe zur
Maschine in eine Lebensform umsetzten und wie Nomaden Streif-

züge durch die USA unternahmen. Die ersten Motorradclubs, und hier vor allem die an der Nordwestküste, wie die Galopping Gooses, die Pegans und die Hells Angels, waren den Hütern der Moral ein Dorn im Auge. Besonders nach der Hollister-Affäre, bei dem eine nie aufgeklärte Vergewaltigung stattgefunden hatte, war es dem jeden und alles verdächtigenden Beamtenapparat von Präsident J. Ed Hoover ein leichtes, Motorradclubs zu kriminalisieren. Denn schließlich präsentierten die Rocker öffentlich ihre Mitgliedschaft und trugen stolz die Farben und Abzeichen ihrer Clubs auf dem Rücken. Vor allem, wenn Wahlen anstanden, kam es zu Prozessen gegen die Biker. Wer Sheriff, Kommissar, Bürgermeister, Senator, Staatsanwalt oder öffentlicher Ankläger werden wollte, ließ unter Beteiligung der Medien spektakuläre Razzien durchführen und unglaublich hohe Kautionen festsetzen. Meistens mußten die Verhafteten nach den Wahlen ohne Anklageerhebung wieder frei-gelassen werden. Bei den Schadensersatzforderungen wurden dann die Steuerzahler zur Kasse gebeten.

Angesichts dieser Hexenjagd beschloß der amerikanische Bund der Motorradfahrer, die zweifelhaften Mitglieder auszuschließen. Motorradfahrern mit Tätowierungen und abgeschnittenen Jeans-jacken wurde die Mitgliedschaft gekündigt; diese kleine Gruppe machte sowieso nur ungefähr ein Prozent der amerikanischen Motorradfahrer aus. Mit großer Belustigung entwarfen sie einen eigenen Aufnäher für die Jacke, den sie auch stolz und provo-zierend als Tätowierung trugen: eine »13« (für M als dreizehnter Buchstabe im Alphabet) stand für Marihuana, und auch Slogans wie »Live to Ride, Ride to Live« waren üblich. Diese Gruppen hatten großen Zulauf. Sie gab eigene Zeitschriften heraus, in denen ihr Lebensgefühl beschrieben wurde, wobei Tätowierungen einen wichtigen Teil ausmachten. Hersteller und Lieferanten von Tätowierzubehör witterten ein lukratives Geschäft und begannen, gezielt für Tätowiermaschinen und anderes zu werben. Wie Pilze schossen die Tattooshops aus dem Boden. Allerdings mangelte es an Informationen über das technische Know-how, das Anordnen und Löten der Nadeln, und es verbreitete sich die Single-Needle-Technik, die ihren Ursprung im Gefängnis hatte. Auch um die bereits bestehende Tätowierkunst wußte die Mehrzahl

der Amateure nichts und bereicherte – oder besser: reduzierte –
die Tradition des Tätowierens mit unsinnigen Motiven, wie zum
Beispiel Burgen. Vereinzelt entwickelten sich talentierte und
lernbegierige Tätowierer weiter, aber eigentlich war es ein amateur-
hafter Stil, dessen baldiges Verschwinden abzusehen war.

Inzwischen gibt es wieder mehr professionelle Tätowierer, und
auch das Publikum ist besser informiert und legt Wert auf
Qualität und fachmännische Beratung. Hochbegabte Illustrations-
künstler faßten erfolgreich Fuß in dem Fach der Tätowierkunst,
wie Bob Roberts, Mike Malone, Jack Rudy und Dave Shore.

Vor allem aber Ed Hardy muß genannt werden, der bei den
Meistern der traditionellen Tätowierung lernte – bei Zeke Owen,
bei Sailor Jerry Collins aus Honolulu und später bei Horihide
Kazuo Oguri aus Gifu in Japan – und einer der größten Tätowierer
aller Zeiten wurde. Er bereicherte die Tattooszene mit der sogenannten Tribal-Tätowierung, die in Motiv und Gestaltung ihren
Ursprung in den traditionellen Tätowierungen primitiver Kulturen,
wie zum Beispiel der Iban und Dayak auf Borneo, hat.

Die Fotos in diesem Buch stammen fast ausschließlich aus dem
Archiv des »Amsterdam Tattoo Museum«.

Das Museum mit Bibliothek, das im Mai 1996 eröffnet wurde,
ist in dieser Form weltweit einzigartig und dokumentiert die
Geschichte der Tätowierung anhand unterschiedlichster Quellen.
Den harten Kern der Bestände bilden die Sammlungen Skuse und
Kobel, die ich wie viele andere Fotosammlungen und Nachlässe
in den letzten 20 Jahren erwerben konnte: Kisten voller Negative,
Originalabzüge, Kopien und natürlich auch Tattookataloge der
letzten fünf Jahrzehnte. Dabei gab es in der Regel für den einzelnen
Abzug einen Einheitspreis; bei Skuse allerdings stieg der Preis,
je mehr von den Geschlechtsteilen abgebildet war. Die meisten
der Fotos in diesem Buch stammen von unbekannten Fotografen,
oftmals von den Tätowierern selber. Diesen sowie allen Modellen
sei an dieser Stelle gedankt.

Henk Schiffmacher

From the Early Days to the 1980s

Circus Posters, about 1900

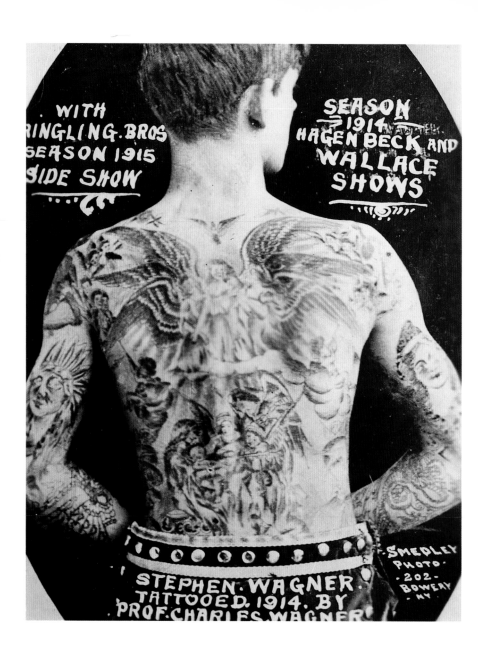

Tattoo: Charles Wagner, New York, USA (New York), 1914

Charles Wagner at Work, New York, USA (New York), 1920s

Deafy and Stelly Grossman, 1920s

Artoria, Circus Lady, 1920s

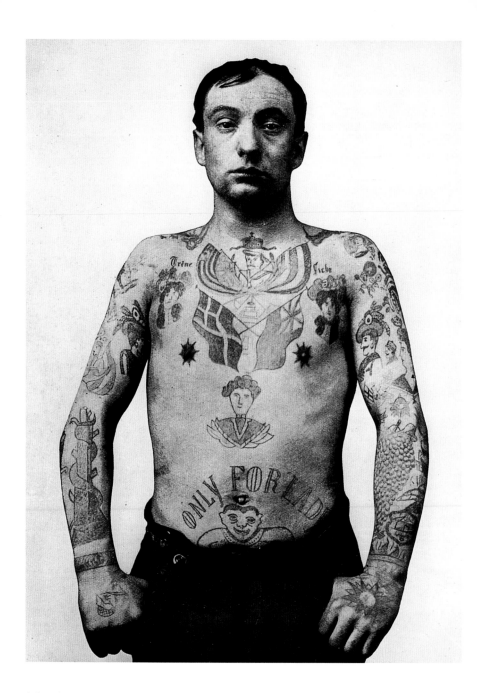

Artist unknown, 1920s

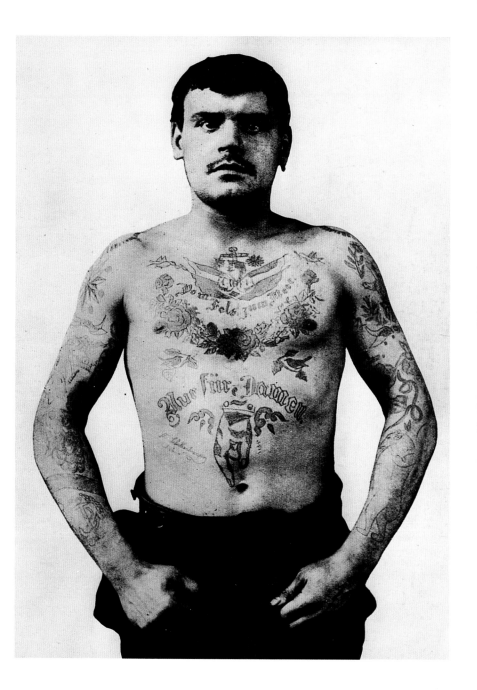

Bert Grim at Work, Los Angeles, USA (California), 1930s

Lotta Pictoria Tattooed by Charles Wagner, New York, USA (New York), 1920s

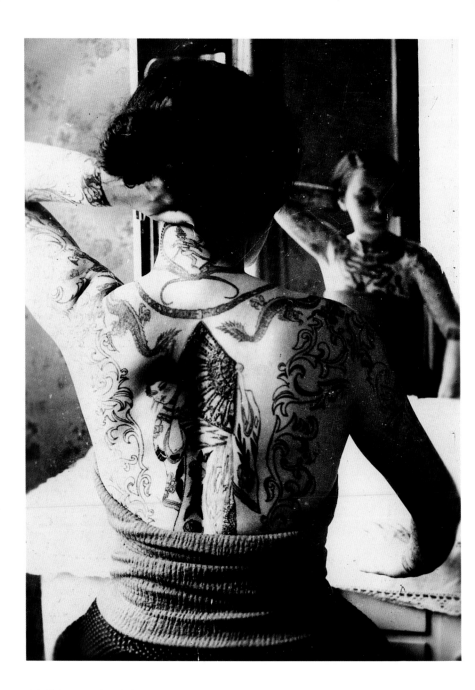

Artist Unknown, early 20th Century

Edith Burchett, London, Great Britain, about 1920

Artist Unknown, early 20th Century

Tattooed Head, 1920s

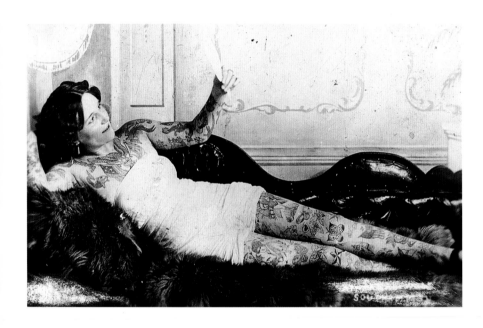

Circus Lady, early 20th Century

La Bella Angora, Tattoo Attraction, Germany, 1920s

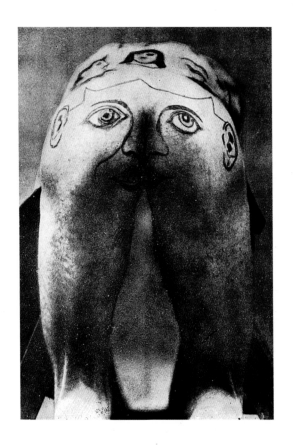

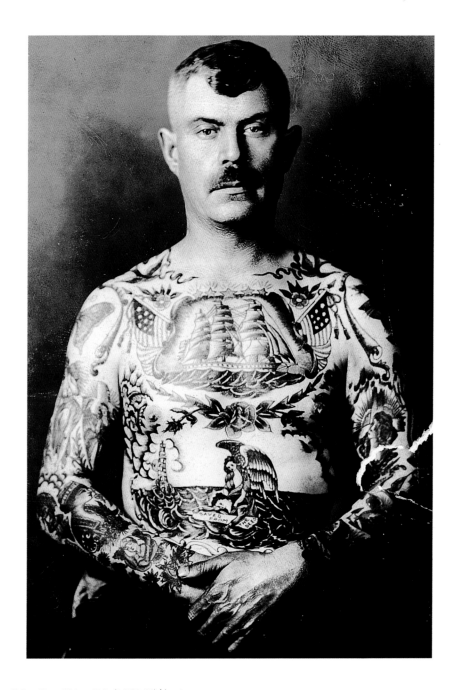

Tattoo: Percy Waters, Detroit, USA (Michigan), 1920s

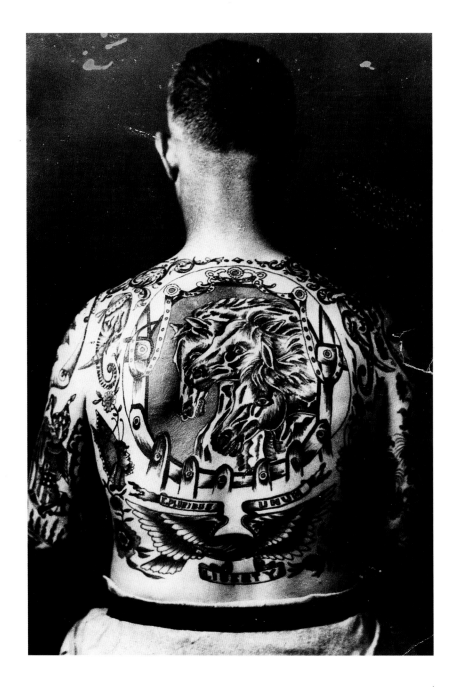

Tattoo: Percy Waters, Detroit, USA (Michigan), 1920s

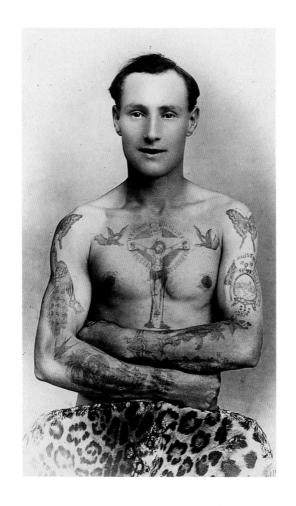

Artist Unknown, 1920s

Tattoo: Percy Waters, Detroit, USA (Michigan), 1920s

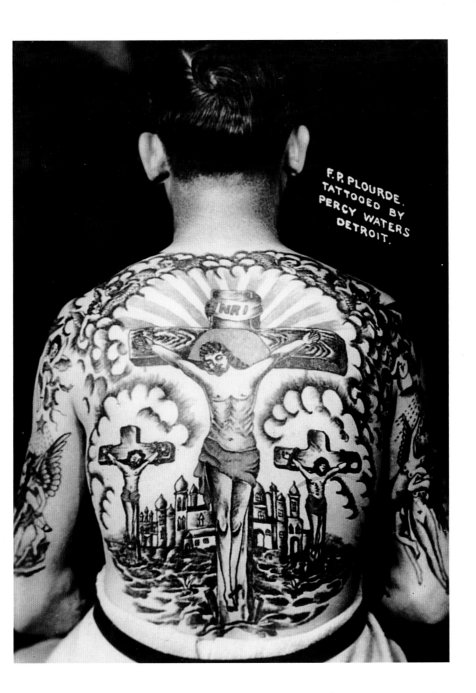

F.P. PLOURDE.
TATTOOED BY
PERCY WATERS
DETROIT.

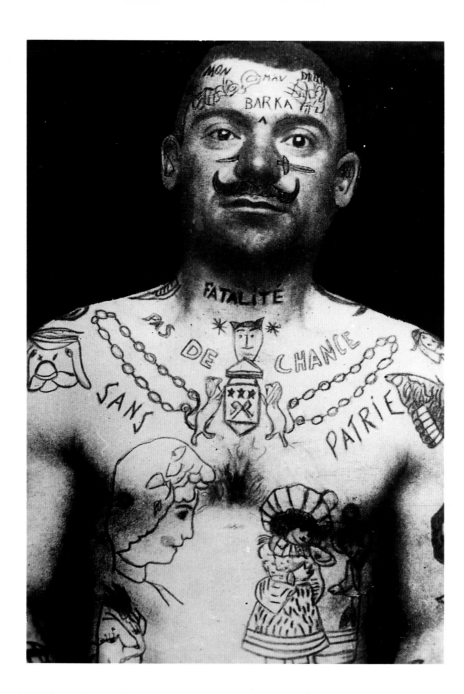

Artist Unknown, France, early 20th Century

Artist Unknown, Great Britain, early 20th Century

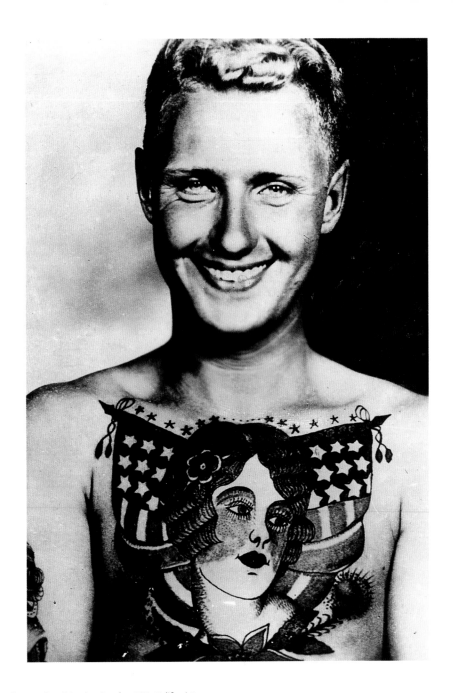

Tattoos: Bert Grim, Los Angeles, USA (California), 1930s

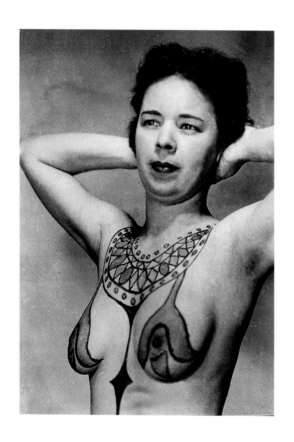

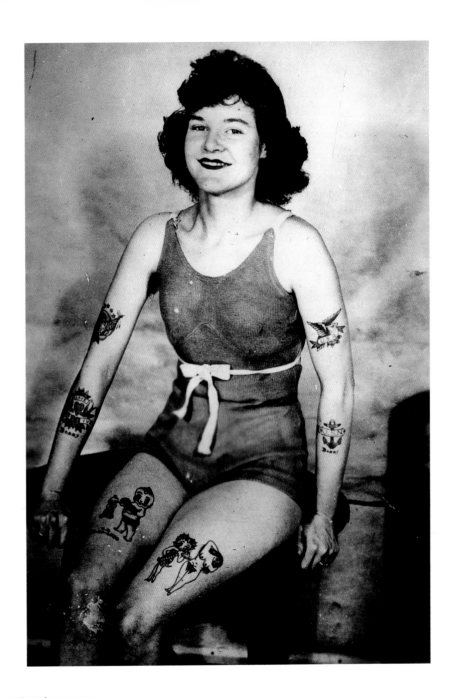

Artist Unknown, 1940s

Artist Unknown, 1950s

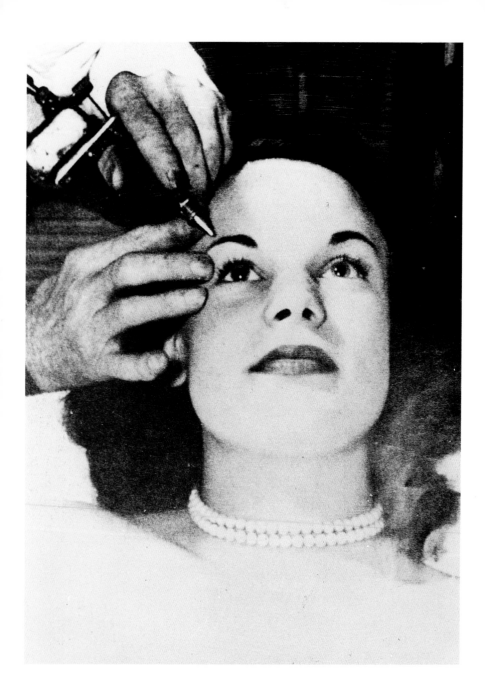

Cosmetic Tattooing, 1940s

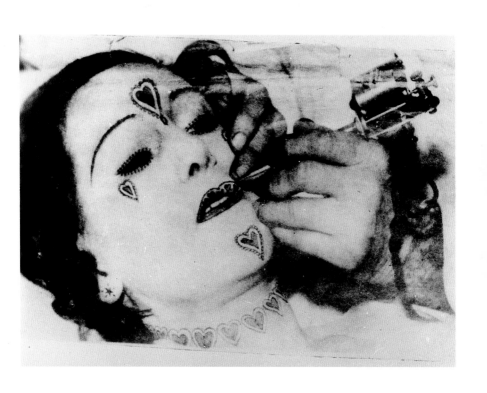

Bob Shaw Tattooed by Bert Grim, Los Angeles, USA (California), 1940s

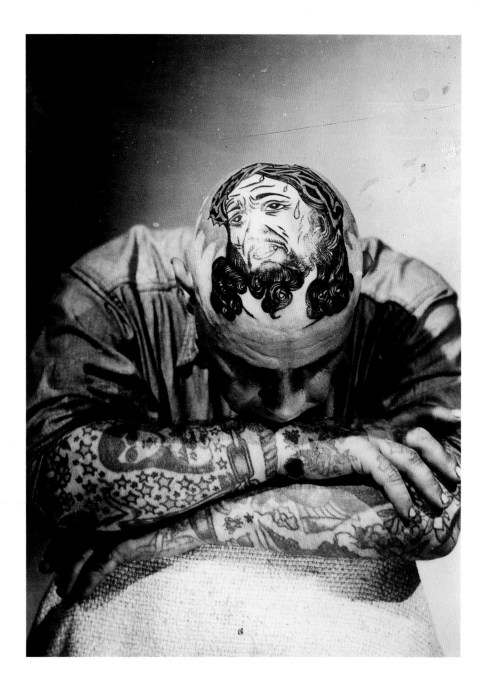

Tattoo: Tatts Thomas, Detroit, USA (Michigan), about 1930

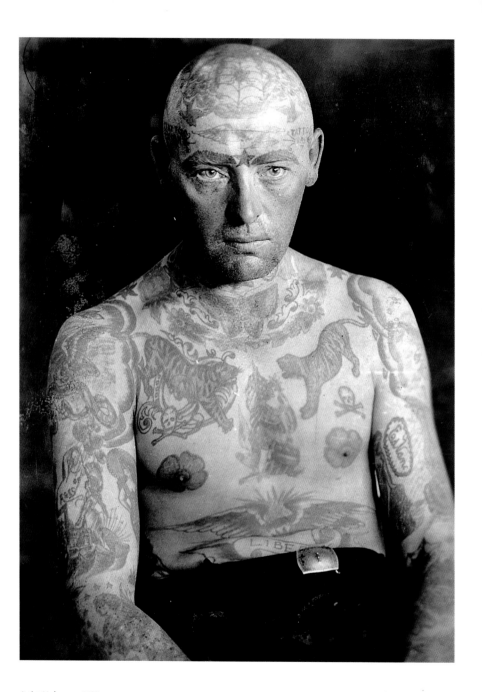

Artist Unknown, USA, 1930s

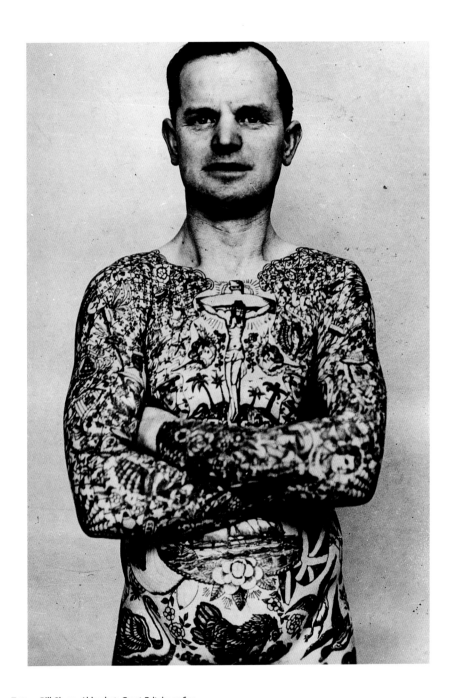

Tattoo: Bill Skuse, Aldershot, Great Britain, 1960s

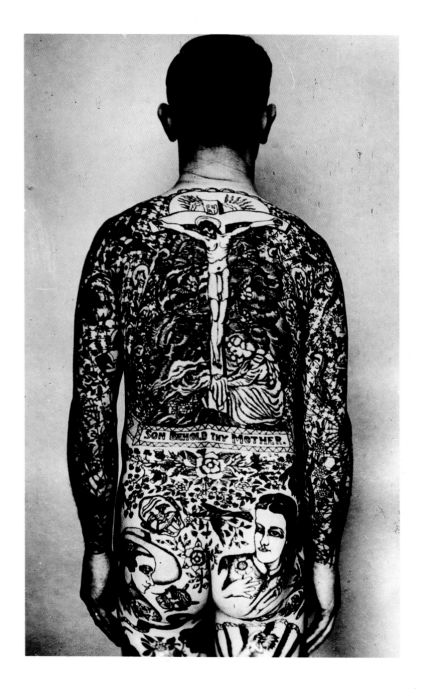

Tattoos: Les Skuse, Bristol, Great Britain, 1950s

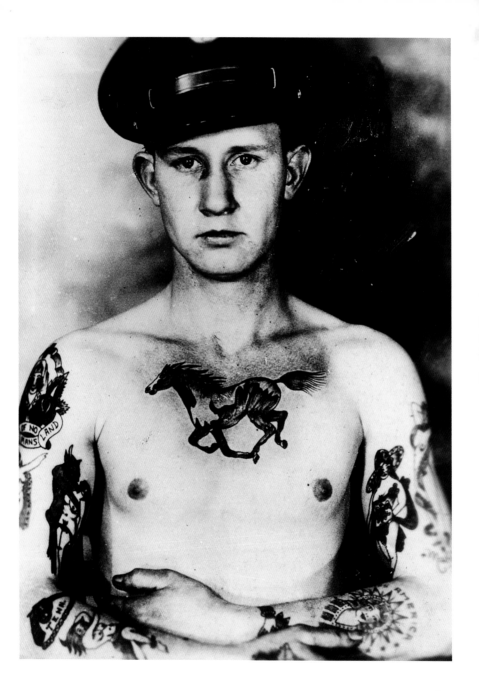

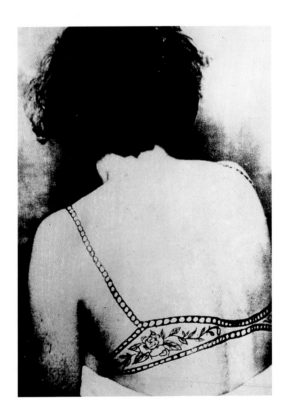

Artist Unknown, 1950s

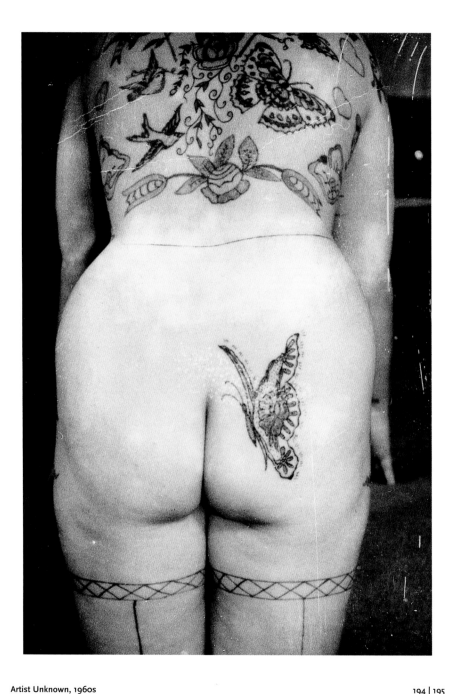

Artist Unknown, 1960s

Ron Ackers at Work, Bristol, Great Britain, 1950s

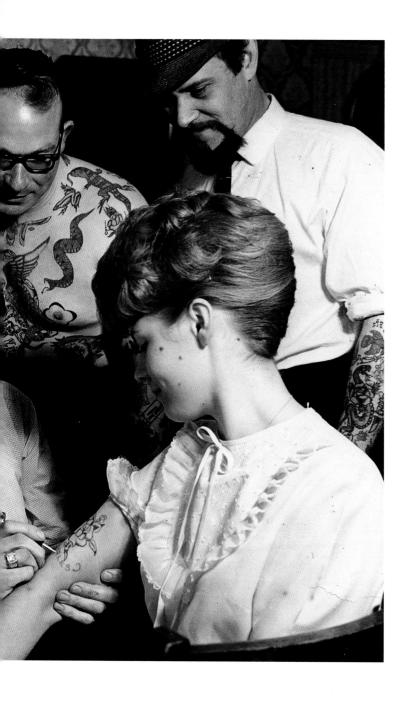

Pamela Nash Tattooed by Les Skuse, Bristol, Great Britain, 1950s

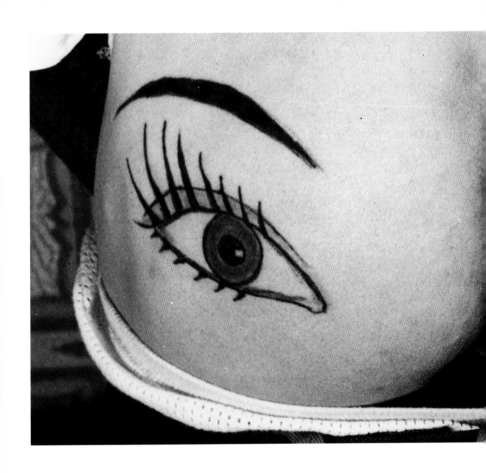

Tattoo: Les Skuse, Bristol, Great Britain, 1950s

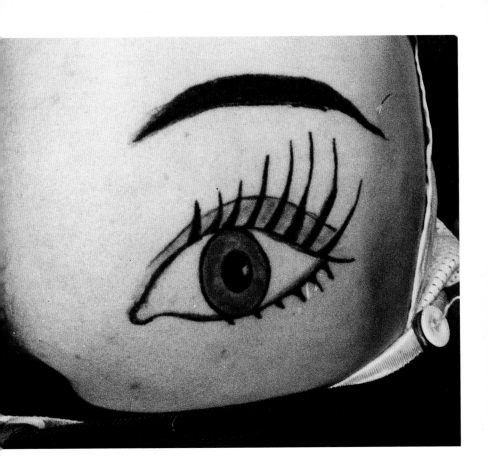

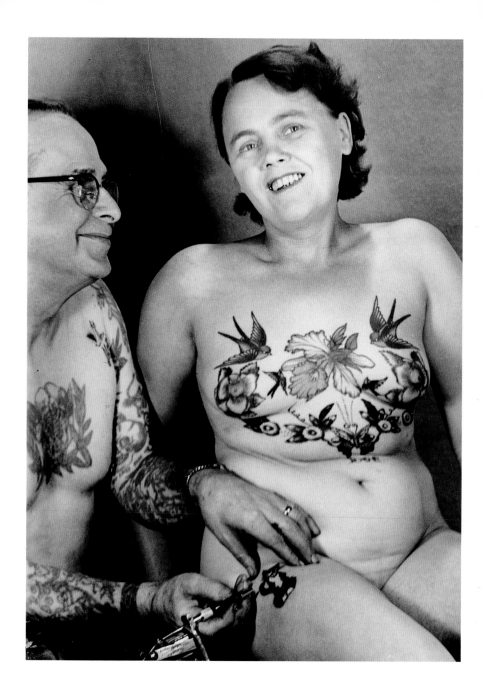

Doc Forbes with Helen, Vancouver, Canada, 1950s

Doc Forbes with Donna, Vancouver, Canada, 1950s

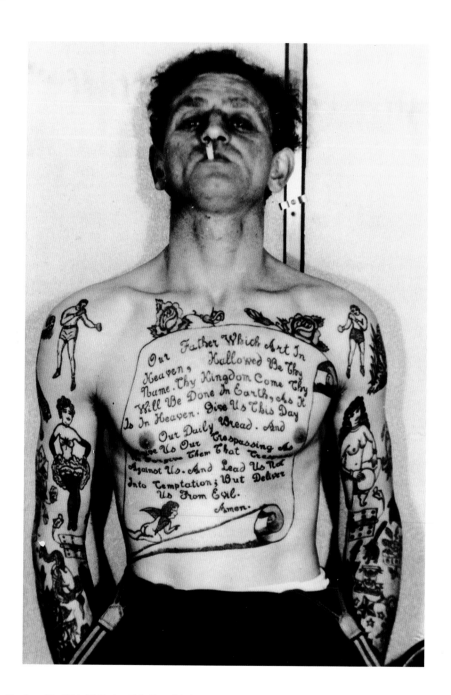

Member of the Bristol Tattooing Club, Great Britain, 1950s

Artist Unknown, 1950s

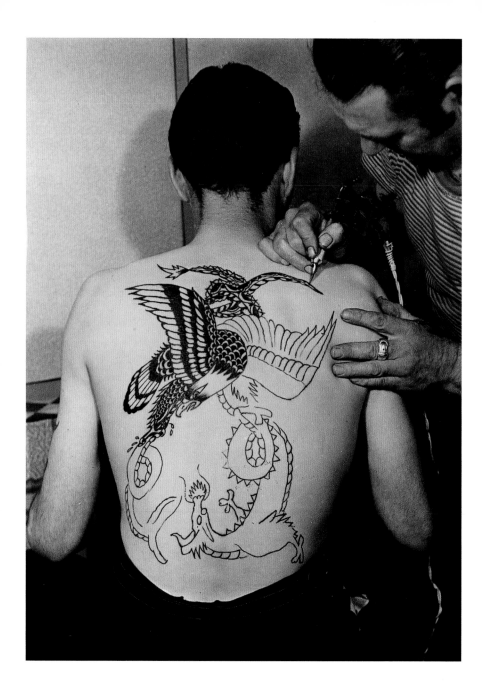

Les Skuse at Work, Bristol, Great Britain, 1950s

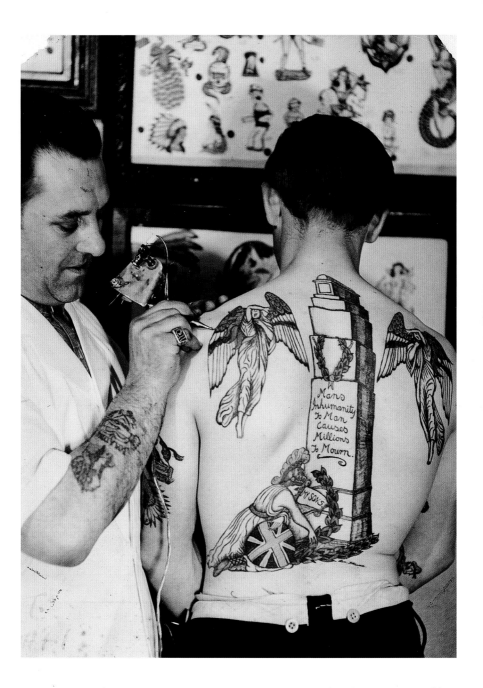

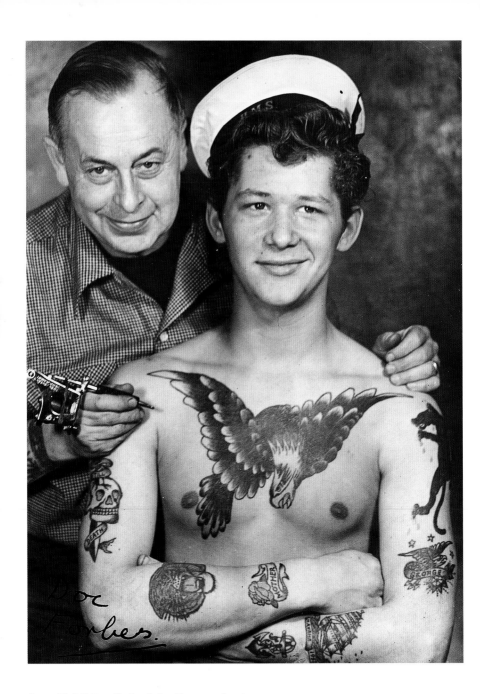

George Whale Tattooed by Doc Forbes, Vancouver, Canada, 1957

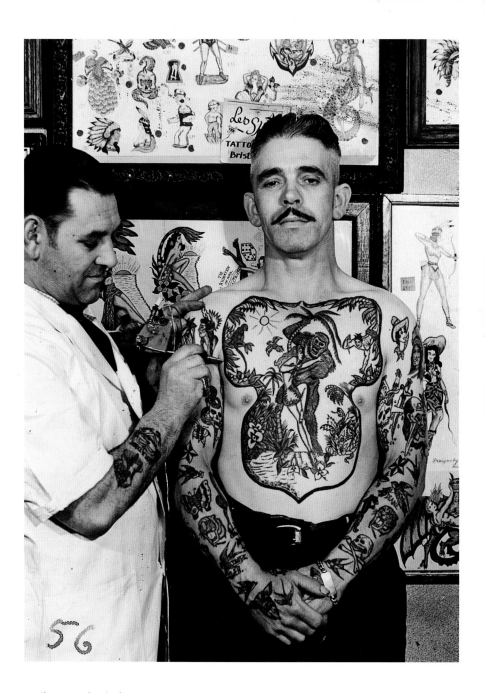

Les Skuse at Work, Bristol, Great Britain, 1950s

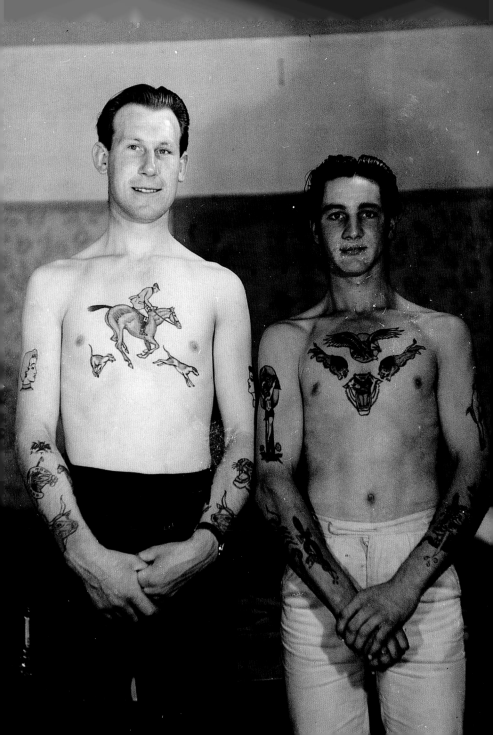

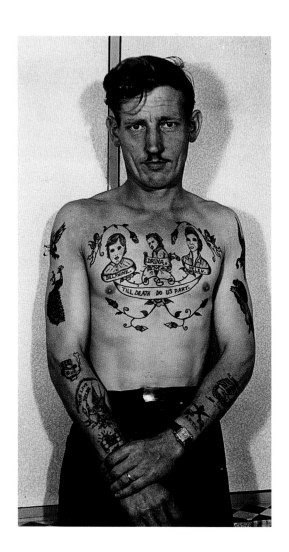

Members of the Bristol Tattooing Club, Great Britain, 1950s

Members of the Bristol Tattooing Club, Great Britain, 1950s

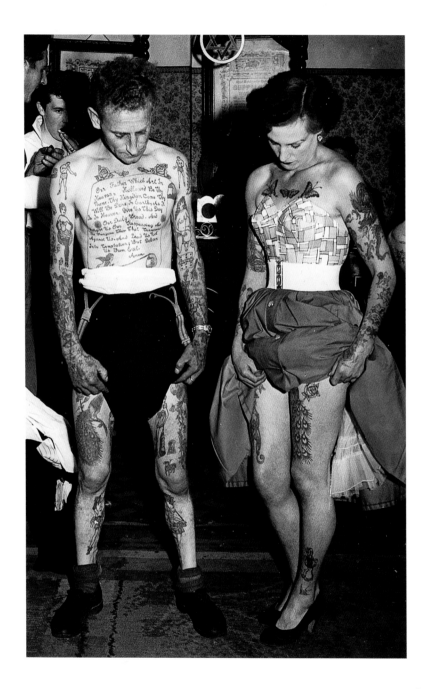

Charles Wagner at Work, New York, USA (New York), 1920s

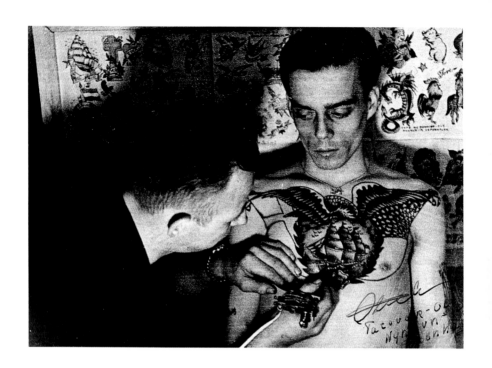

"Tatovør" Ole Hansen at Work, Copenhagen, Denmark, 1950s

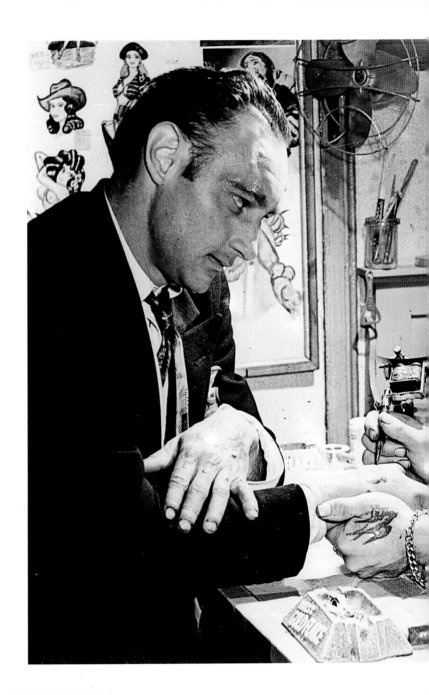

Les Skuse at Work, Bristol, Great Britain, 1950s

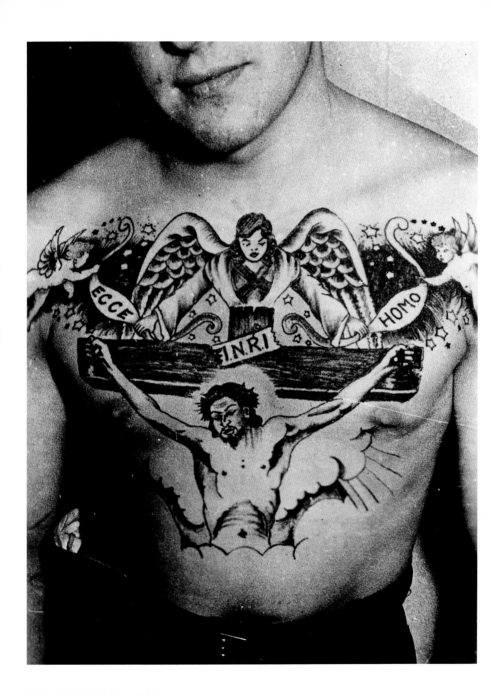

Tattoo: Joe Pancho, Antwerp, Belgium, 1950s

Members of the Bristol Tattooing Club, Great Britain, 1950s

Peter Schulz & Theodor Vetter. Tattoos by Herbert Hoffmann, Hamburg, Germany, about 1965,
Photo: Herbert Hoffmann

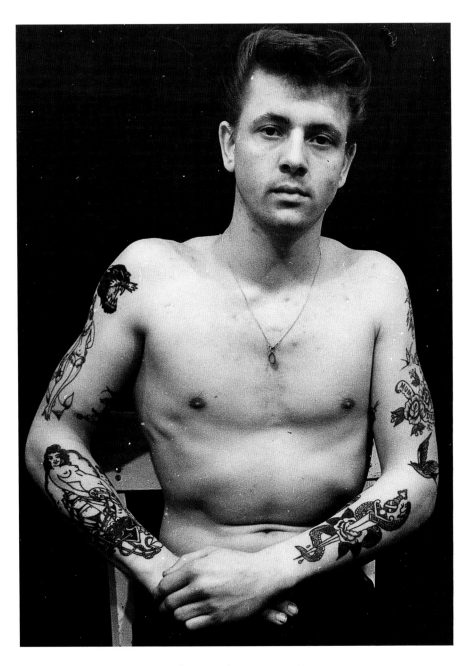

Günther Lohmann. Tattoos by Herbert Hoffmann, Hamburg, Germany, 1966,
Photo: Herbert Hoffmann

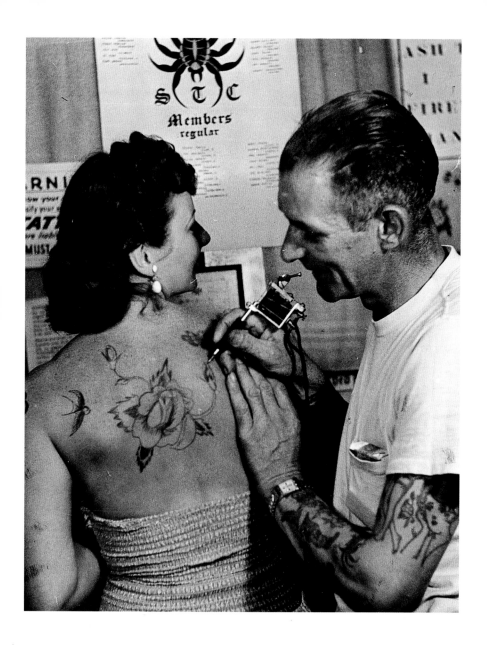

Al Shieferly at Work, USA (Ohio), 1950s

Les Skuse and Al Shieferly at Work, Bristol, Great Britain, 1950s

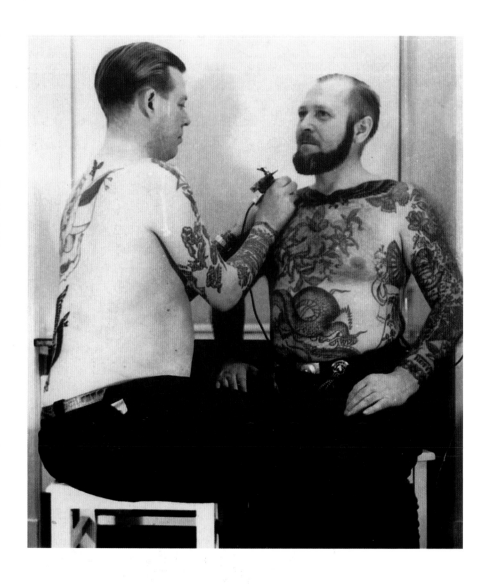

"Tattoo Peter" (Peter de Haan, Amsterdam) & Herbert Hoffmann, Hamburg, Germany, about 1962
Photo: Collection Herbert Hoffmann

Herbert Hoffmann. Tattoos by Christian Warlich, Tattoo Peter, Tatovør Ole, Horst Streckenbach
et als., Heiden, Switzerland, about 1958, Photo: Collection Herbert Hoffmann

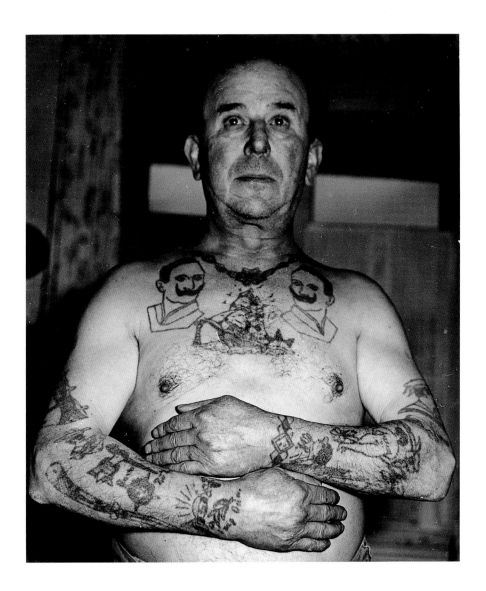

Hermann Rössler, Düsseldorf, Germany, 1957, Photo: Herbert Hoffmann

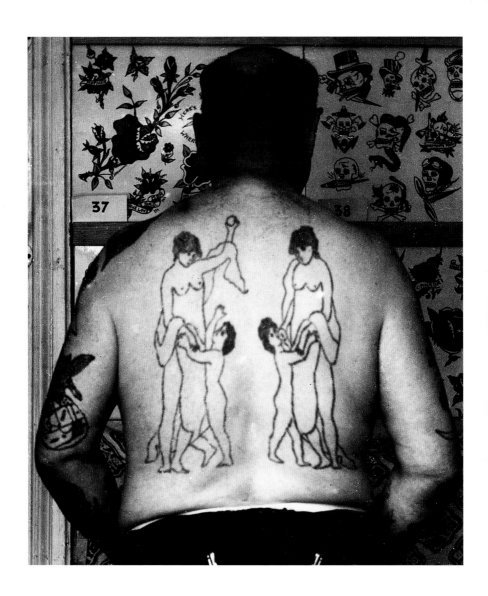

Willy Brandt, Hamburg, Germany, about 1957, Photo: Herbert Hoffmann

Tattoo: Les Skuse, Bristol, Great Britain, 1960

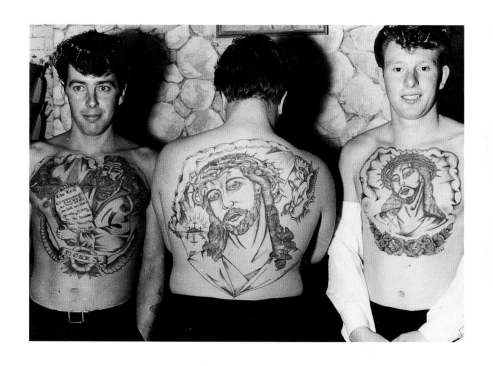

Tattoos: Bill Skuse, Aldershot, Great Britain, 1960s

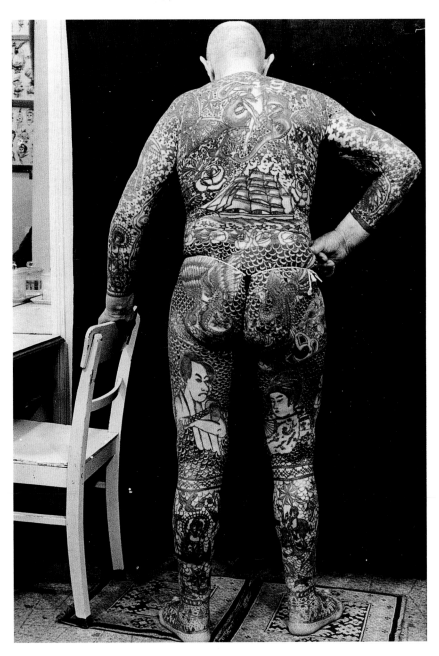

Wilhelm Wedekemper. Tattoos by Blumberg, Kuchenbäcker, Christian Warlich & Herbert Hoffmann, Hamburg, Germany, 1960s, Photo: Herbert Hoffmann

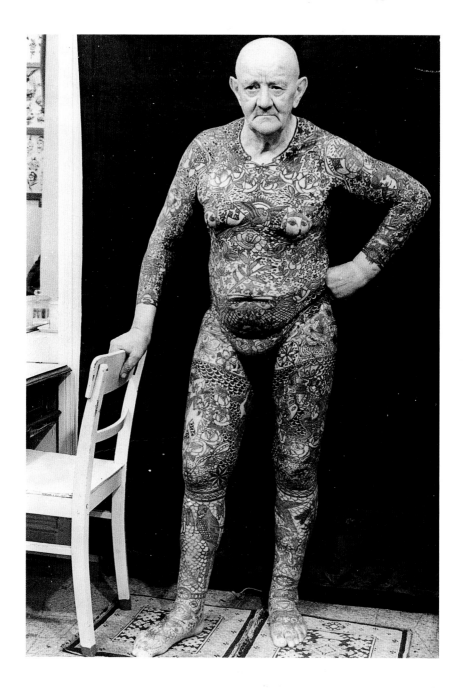

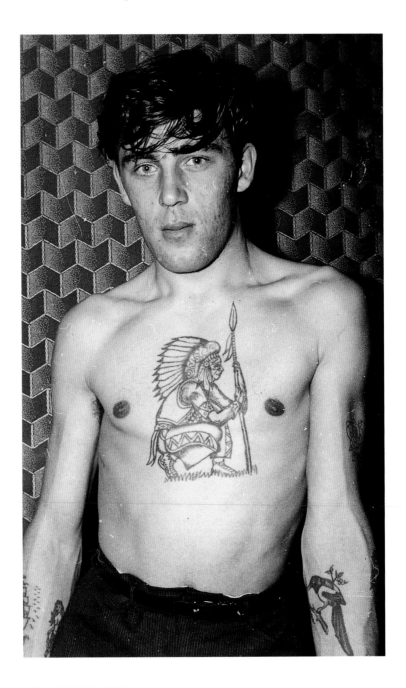

Tattoo: Les Skuse, Bristol, Great Britain, 1950s

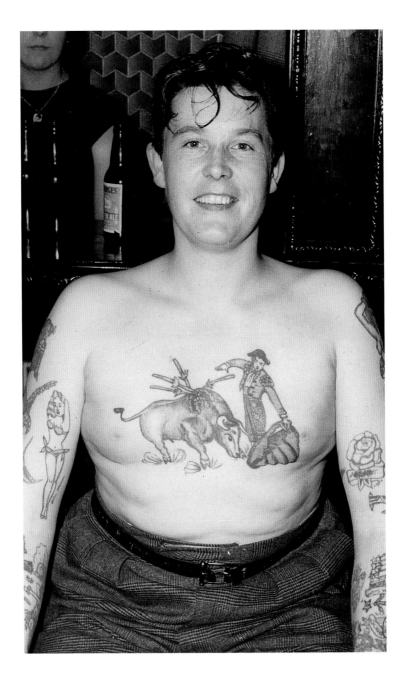

Ron Ackers, Bristol, Great Britain, 1950s

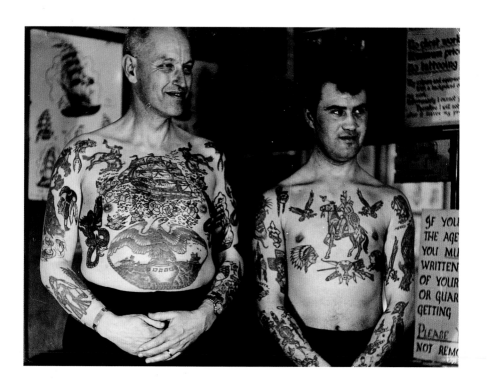

Members of the Bristol Tattooing Club, Great Britain, 1960s

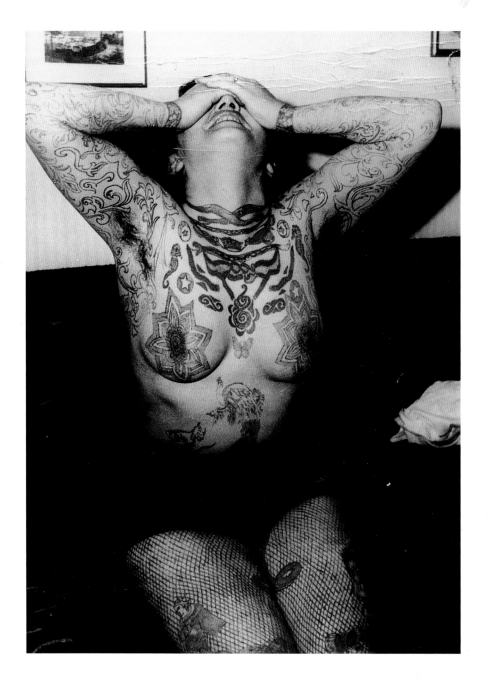

Artist Unknown, 1950s

Tattoo: Les Skuse, Bristol, Great Britain, 1960s

International Tattoo Convention, Bristol, Great Britain, 1950

Ron Ackers at Work, Bristol, Great Britain, 1950s

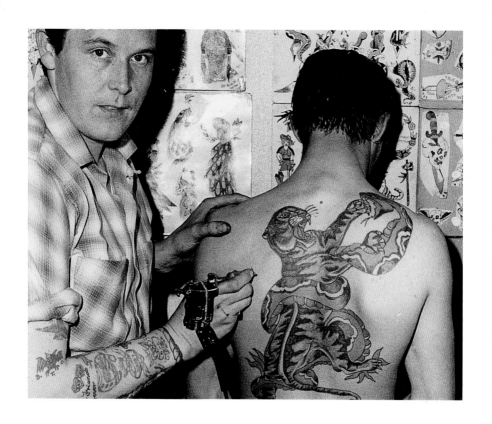

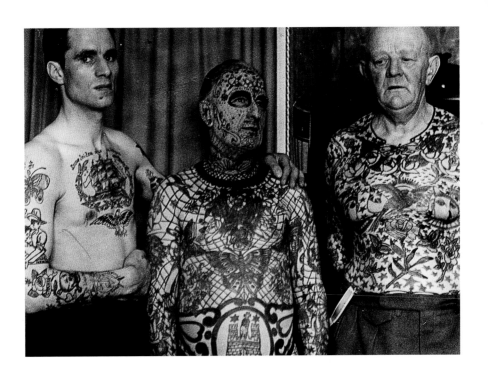

Theo Vetter, Karl Oergel, Wilhelm Wedekämper. Tattoos by Blumberg, Kuchenbäcker, Christian Warlich &
Herbert Hoffmann, Hamburg, Germany, about 1965, Photo: Herbert Hoffmann

Tattoos: Les Skuse, Bristol, Great Britain, 1950s

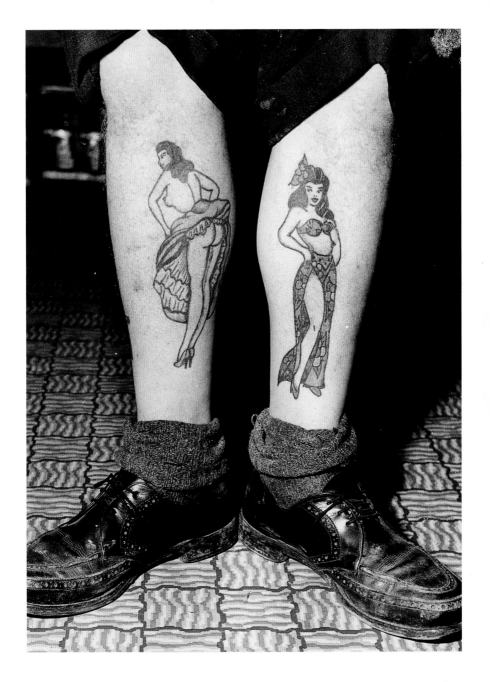

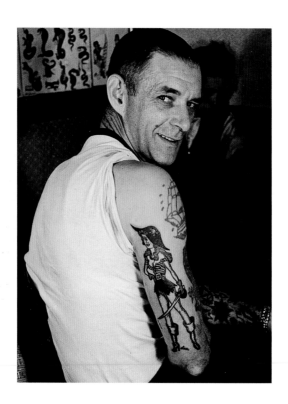

Al Shieferly, USA (Ohio) at the International Tattoo Convention, Bristol, Great Britain, 1950

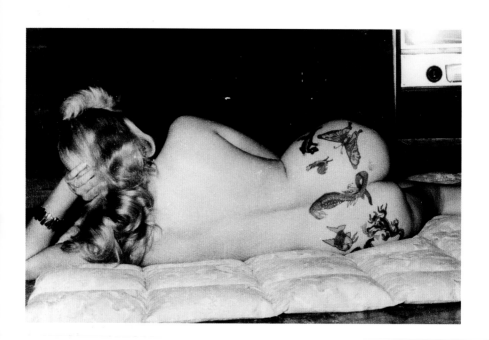

Artist Unknown, 1960s

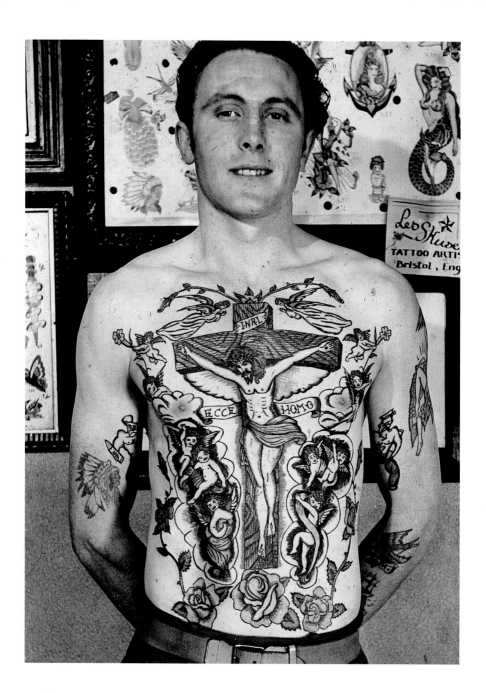

Ron Allen Tattooed by Les Skuse, Bristol, Great Britain, 1960s

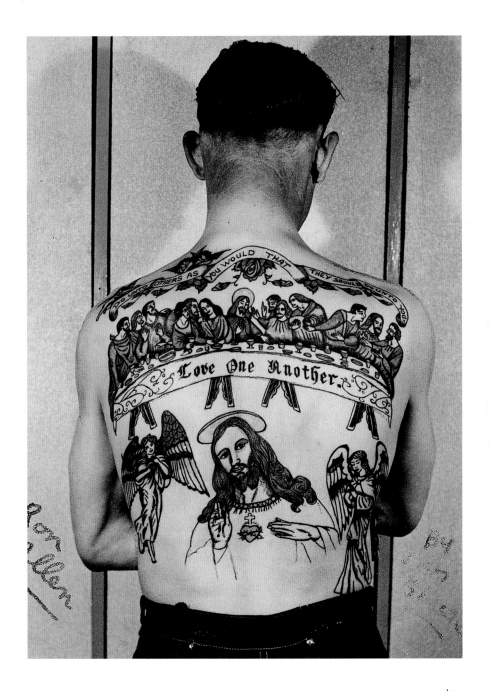

Tattoo: Tattoo Peter at Work, Amsterdam, The Netherlands, 1960s

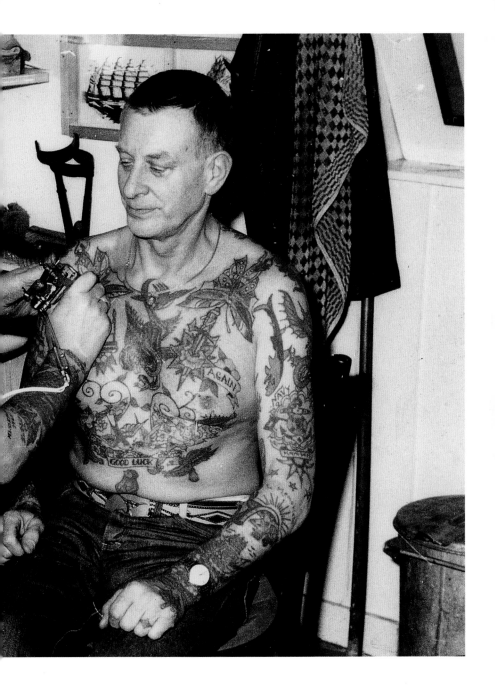

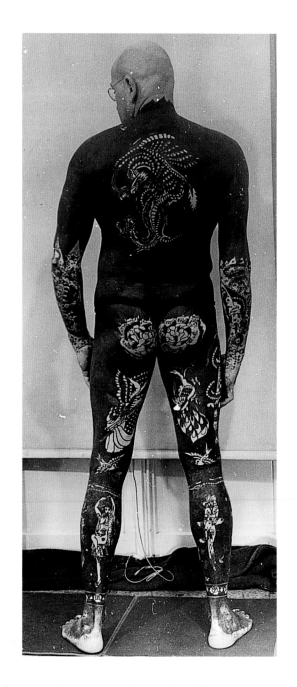

Henry Riedel Jahn (from New York), Germany, 1965, Photo: Herbert Hoffmann

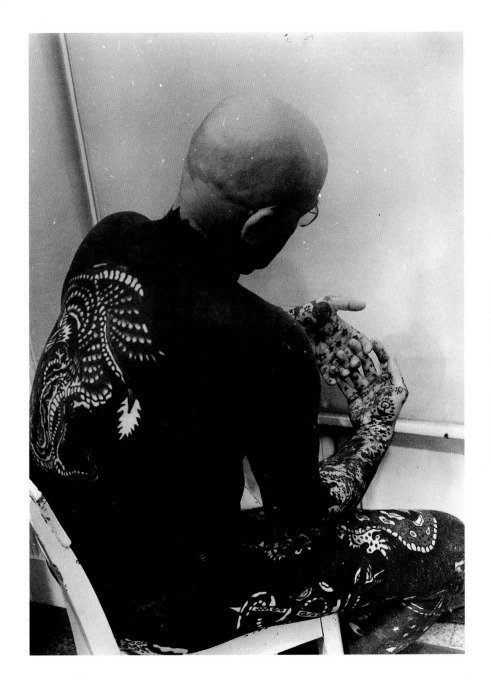

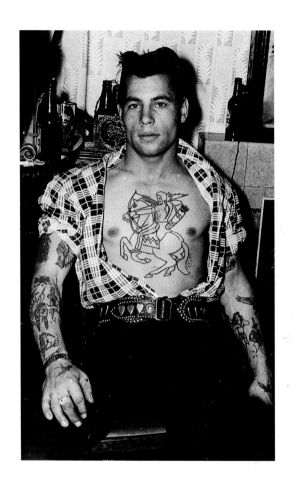

Tattoo: Les Skuse, Bristol, Great Britain, 1960s

Artist Unknown, 1960s

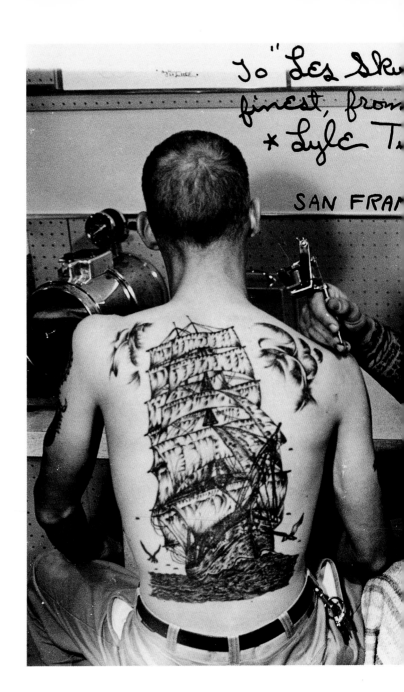

Lyle Tuttle at Work, San Francisco, USA (California), 1960s

é, the

dé *

isco

Artist Unknown, Australia, 1960s

Member of the Bristol Tattooing Club, Great Britain, 1950s

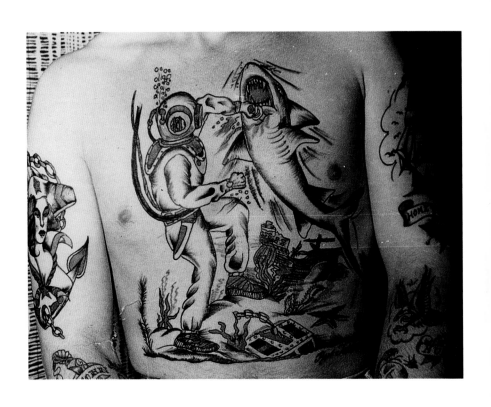

Herbert Hoffmann. Tattoos by Christian Warlich, Tattoo Peter, Tatovør Ole, Horst Streckenbach et als., Heiden, Switzerland, about 1958, Photo: Collection Herbert Hoffmann

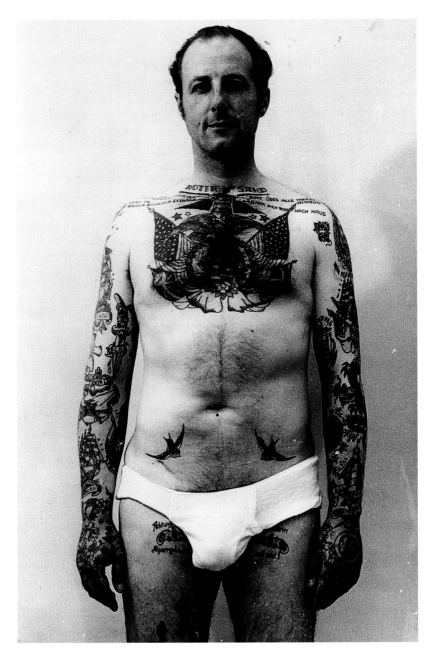

Herbert Krüger. Tattoos by Paul Holzhaus, Albert Heinze & Herbert Hoffmann,
Hamburg, Germany, 1965, Photo: Herbert Hoffmann

Doc Forbes and Bunny, Vancouver, Canada, 1960s

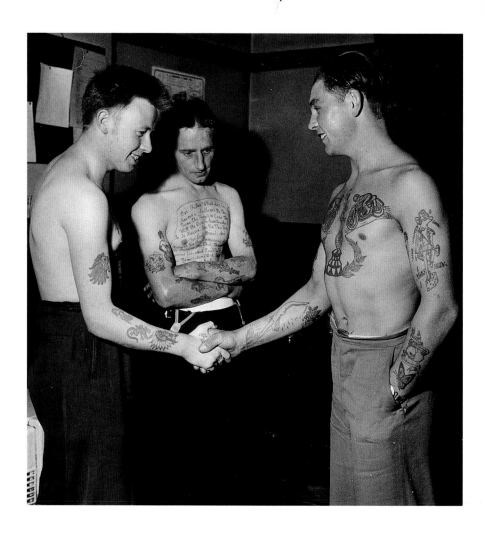

Mewmbers of the Bristol Tattooing Club, Great Britain, 1960s

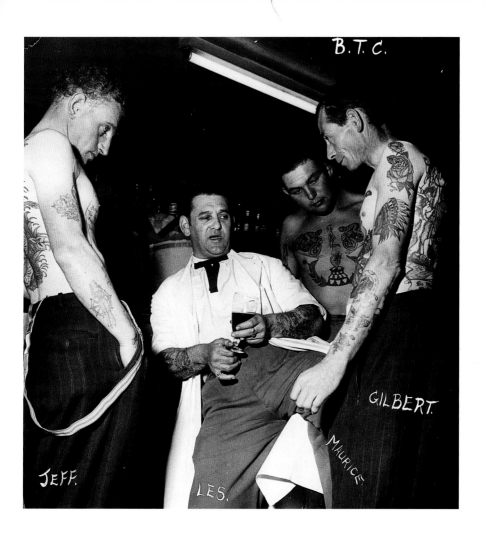

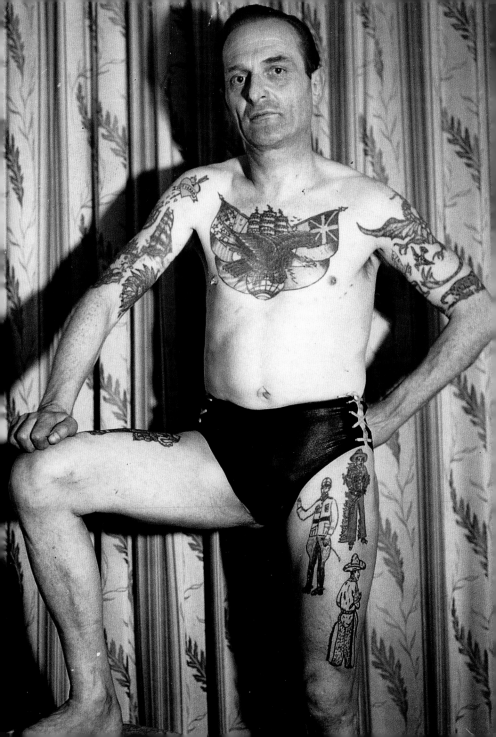

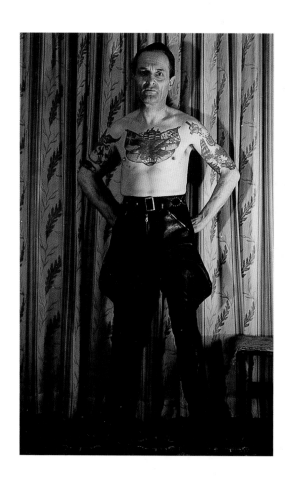

Kurtz Wutzdorf. Tattoos by Herbert Hoffmann, Berlin, Germany, 1960, Photo: Herbert Hoffmann

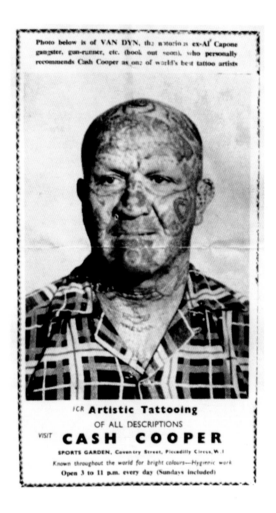

Photo below is of VAN DYN, the notorious ex-Al Capone gangster, gun-runner, etc. (book out soon), who personally recommends Cash Cooper as one of world's best tattoo artists

FOR **Artistic Tattooing**
OF ALL DESCRIPTIONS
VISIT **CASH COOPER**
SPORTS GARDEN, Coventry Street, Piccadilly Circus, W.1
Known throughout the world for bright colours—Hygienic work
Open 3 to 11 p.m. every day (Sundays included)

Van Dyn Tattooed by Cash Cooper, London, Great Britain, 1960s

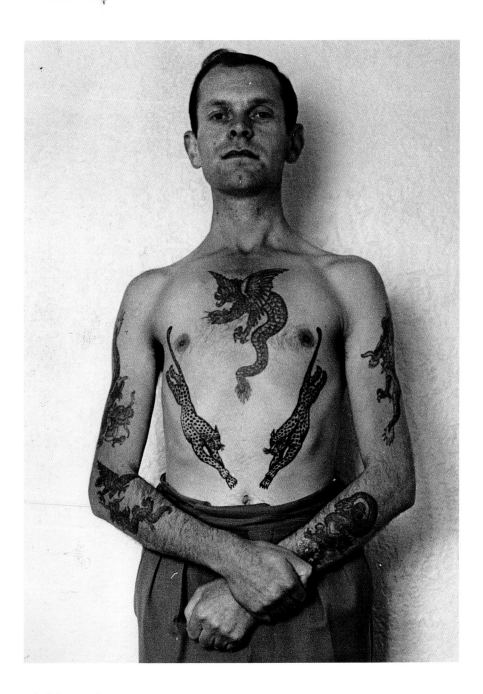

Artist Unknown, 1960s

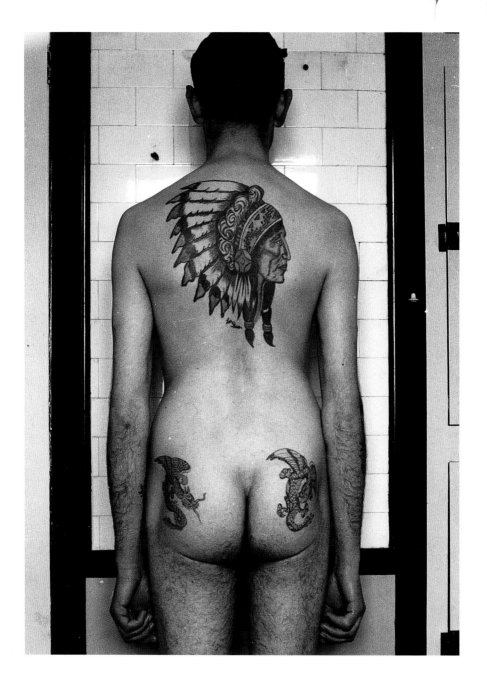

Tattoo, Les Skuse, Bristol, Great Britain, 1960s

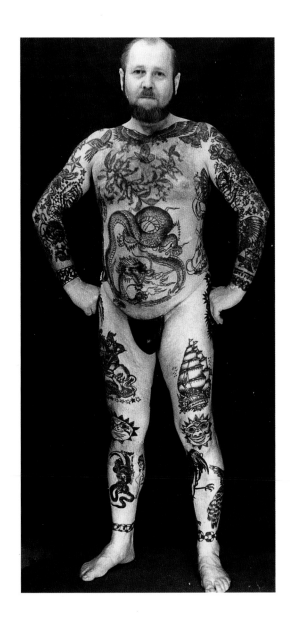

Herbert Hoffmann. Tattoos by Christian Warlich, Tattoo Peter, Tatovør Ole, Horst Streckenbach et als.,
Hamburg, Germany, about 1962, Photo. Collection Herbert Hoffmann

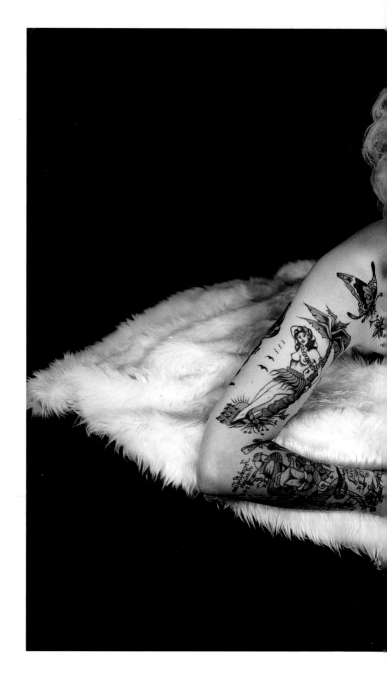

Cindy Ray, Ivanhoe, Australia, 1960s

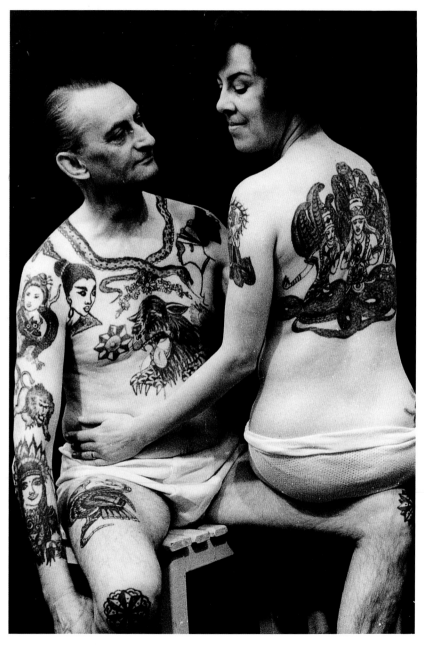

Richard Wulkow & wife. Tattoos by Christian Warlich & Herbert Hoffmann, Hamburg, Germany, about 1965
Photo: Herbert Hoffmann

Bobby Zach & wife, Hamburg, Germany, 1966, Photo: Herbert Hoffmann

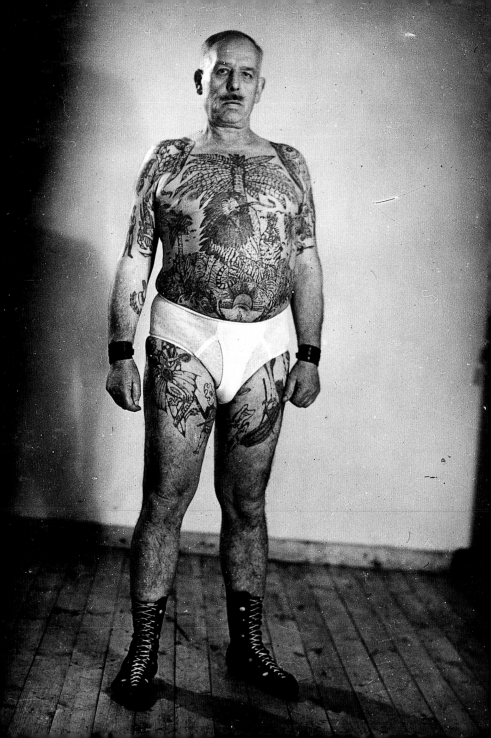

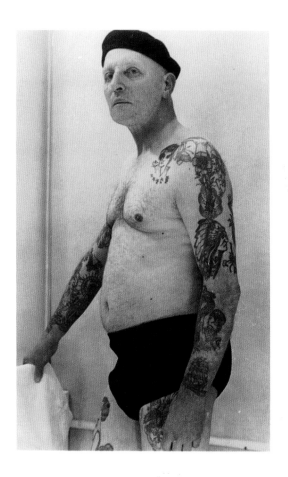

Karl Lente. Tattoos by Christian Warlich & Herbert Hoffmann, Hamburg, Germany, 1963
Photo: Herbert Hoffmann

Valentin Huthöfer, Mainz, Germany, about 1955, Photo: Herbert Hoffmann

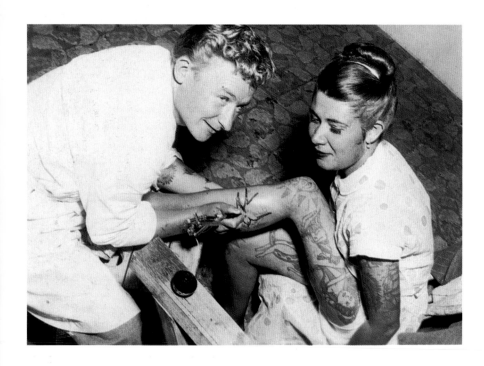

Kevin Davis at Work, 1960s

Rosemarie Squire Tattooing Les Skuses, Bristol, Great Britain, 1960

Members of the Bristol Tattooing Club, Great Britain, 1950s

Gilbert
Milsom.

B.T.C.

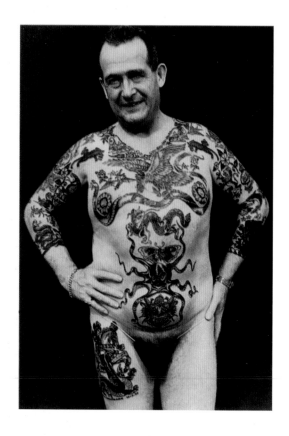

Niels Tuxen (from Denmark). Tattoos by Huck Spaulding, Sailor Eddie, Paul Rogers, Cliff Raven, Hamburg, Germany, 1965, Photo: Herbert Hoffmann

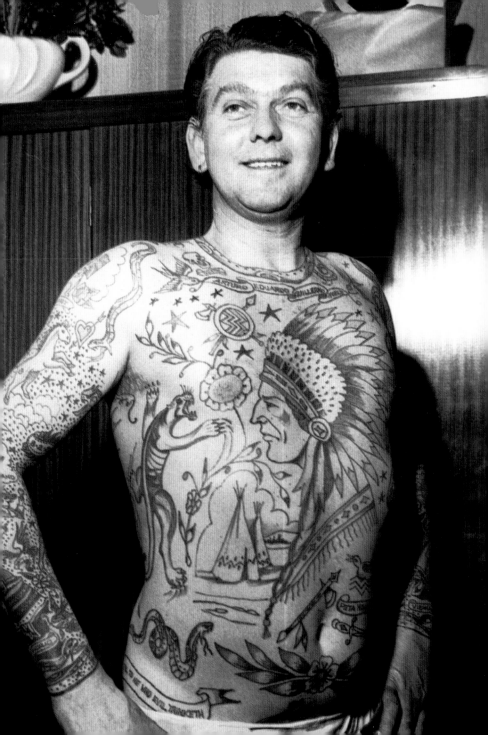

Pamela Nash Tattooed by Les Skuse, Bristol, Great Britain, 1950s

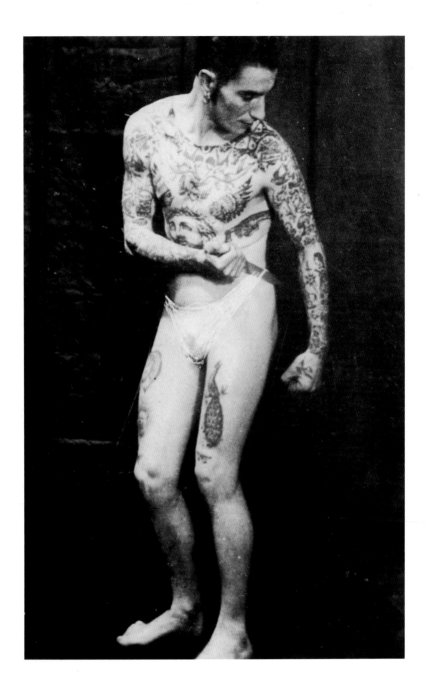

Artist Unknown, 1960s

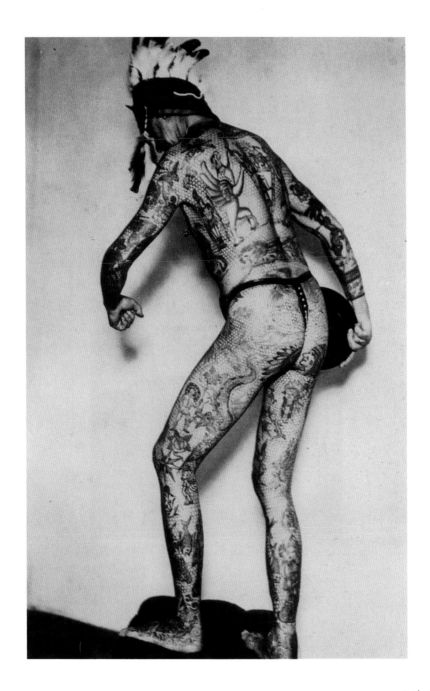

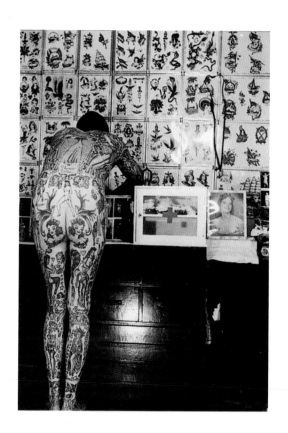

Doc Forbes' Studio, Vancouver, Canada, 1960s

DRAWN TO ORDER by
Doc Forbes

Artist Unknown, Australia, 1960s

Tattoo: Cindy Ray, Ivanhoe, Australia, 1960s

Les Skuses at Work, Bristol, Great Britain, 1960s

Cindy Ray in her Studio, Ivanhoe, Australia, 1960s

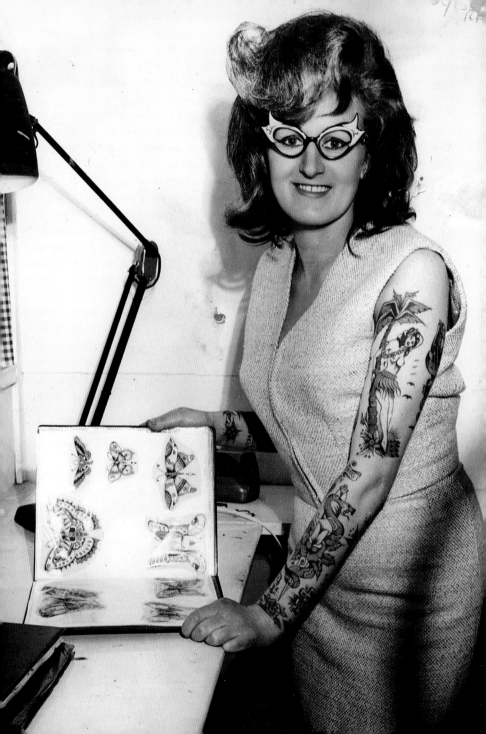

Cindy Ray, Ivanhoe, Australia, 1960s

Tattoo: Cindy Ray, Ivanhoe, Australia, 1960s

Les Skuses in his Studio, Bristol, Great Britain, 1960s

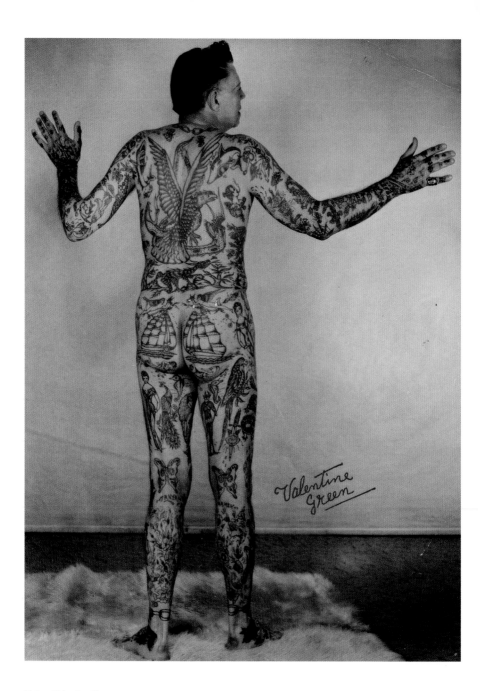

Tattoo: Valentine Green, 1970s

Valentine Green

Artist Unknown, Great Britain, 1970s

Artist Unknown, Great Britain, 1970s

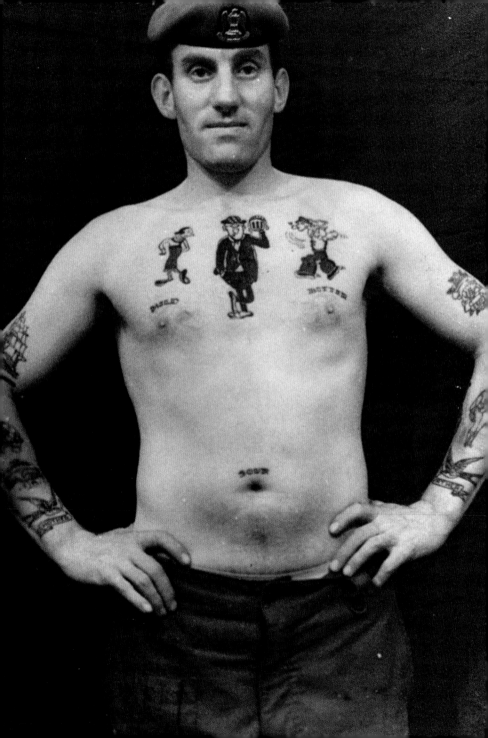

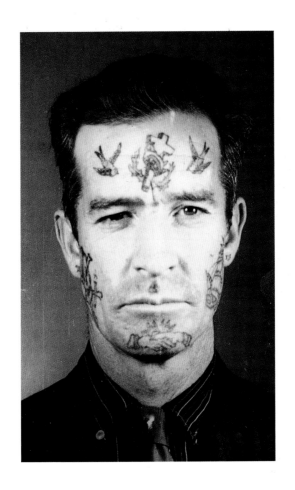

Artist Unknown, 1960s

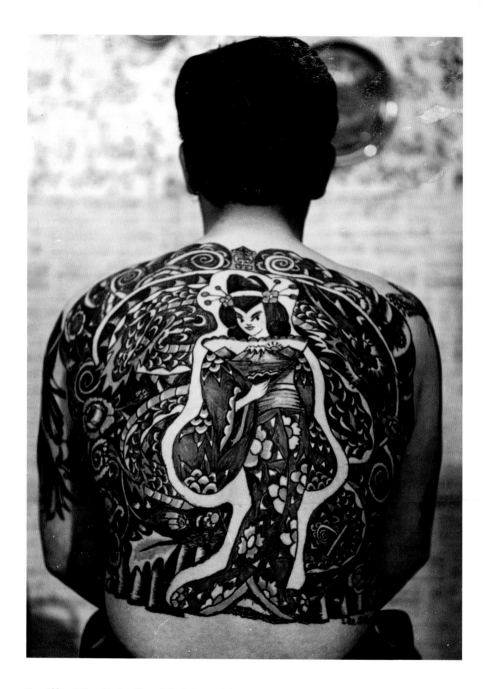

Tony Aldam Tattooed by Les Skuse, Bristol, Great Britain, 1970s

Tattoos: Bill Skuse, Aldershot, Great Britain, 1970s

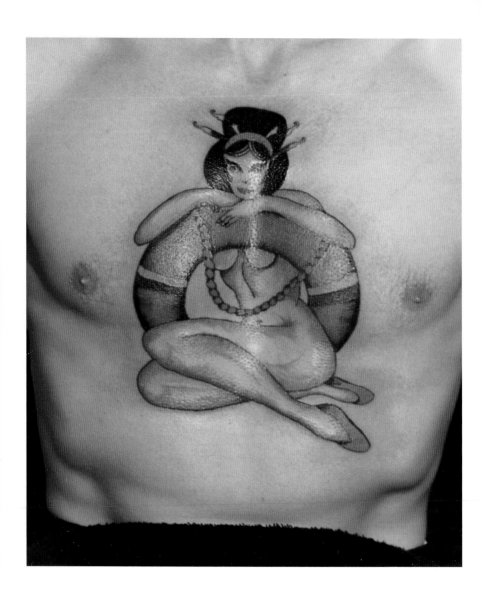

Artist Unknown, 1970s

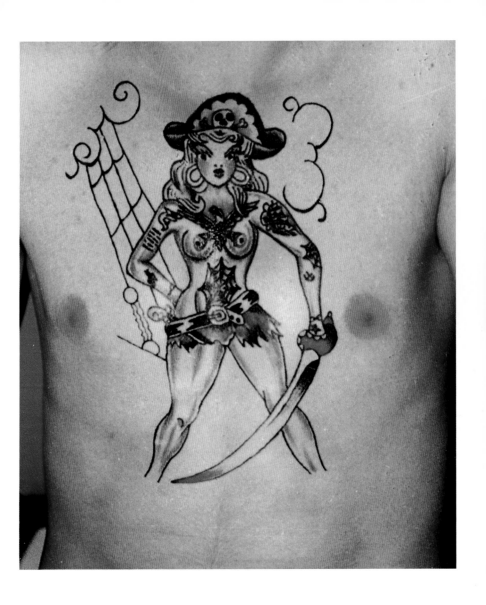

Tattoo: Doc Forest, Stockholm, Sweden, 1970s

Tattoo: Martin Robson, San Diego, USA (California), 1970s

Tattoo: Tattoo Peter, Amsterdam, The Netherlands, 1970s

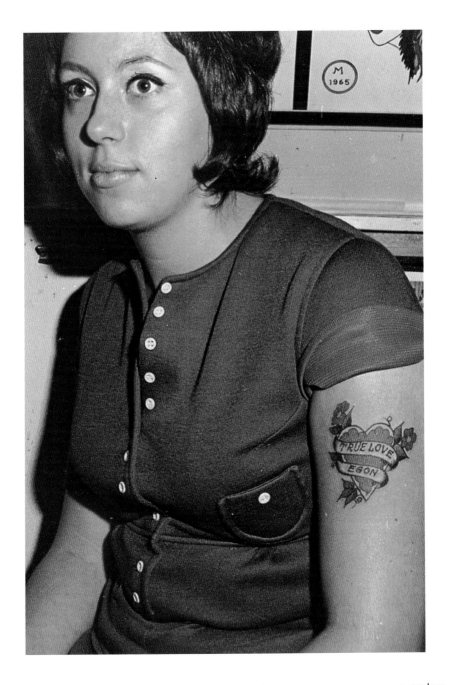

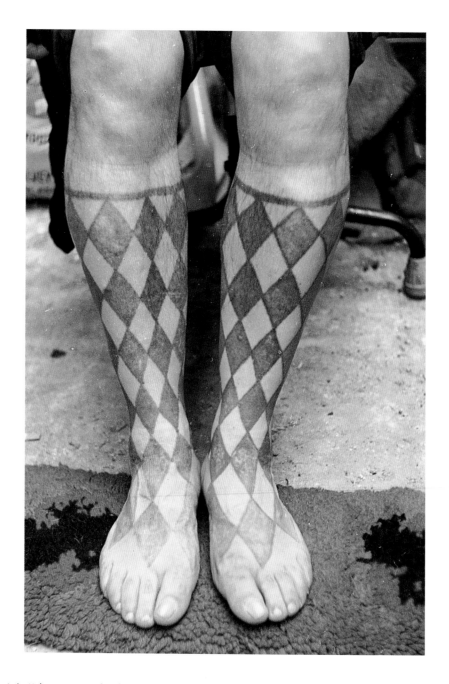

Artist Unknown (Tattooed Socks), 1970s

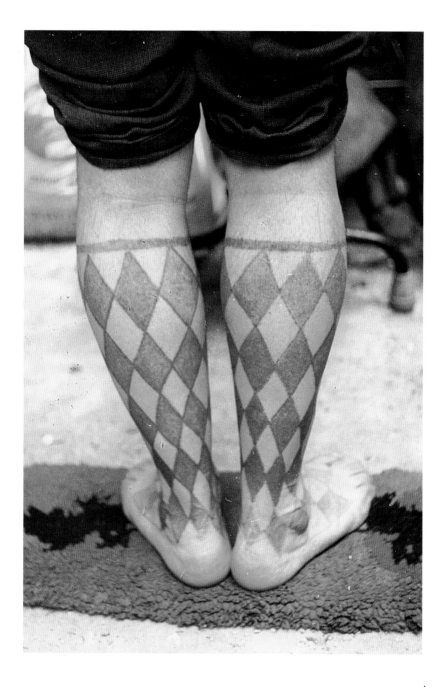

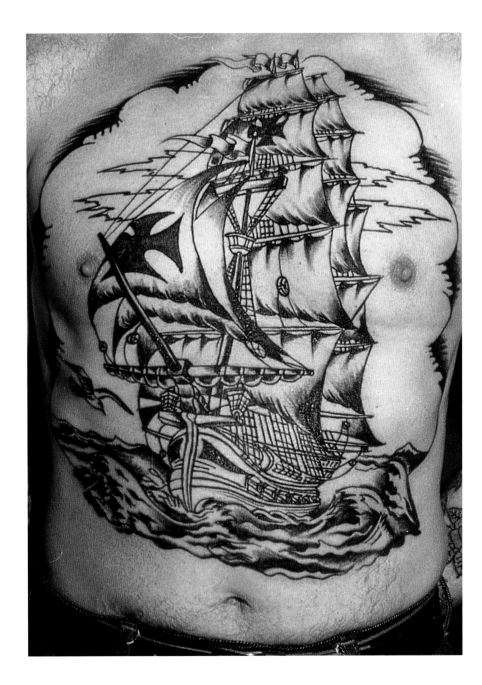

Karl Hermann Richter, Hamburg, Germany, 1974, Photo: Herbert Hoffmann

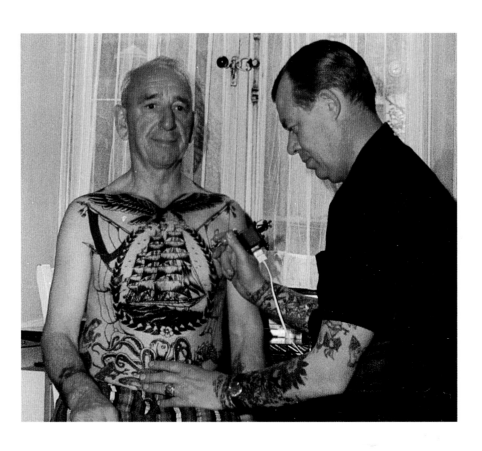

Tattoo Peter (Amsterdam) tattooing Franz Kranwertvogel in Hamburg 1974, Photo: Herbert Hoffmann

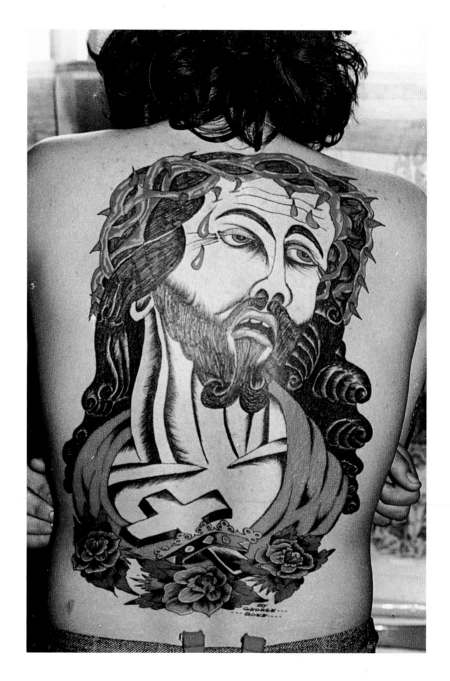

Tattoo: George Bone, London, Great Britain, 1970s

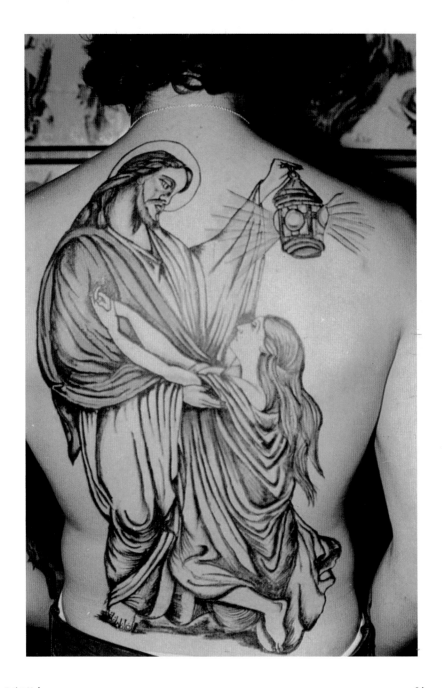

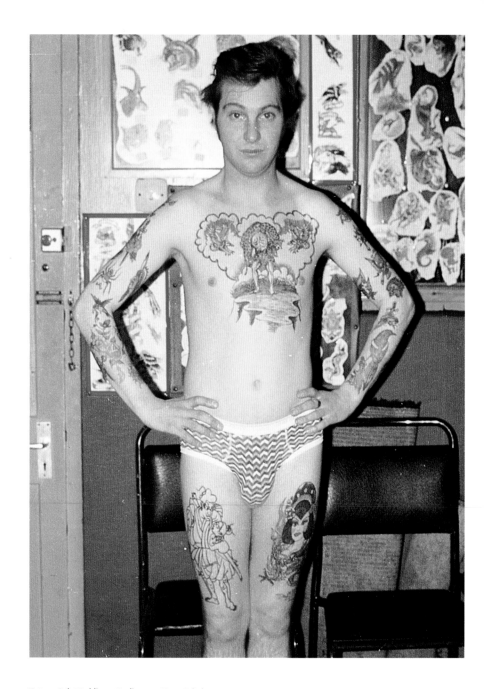

Tattoo: Bob Maddison, Darlington, Great Britain, 1970s

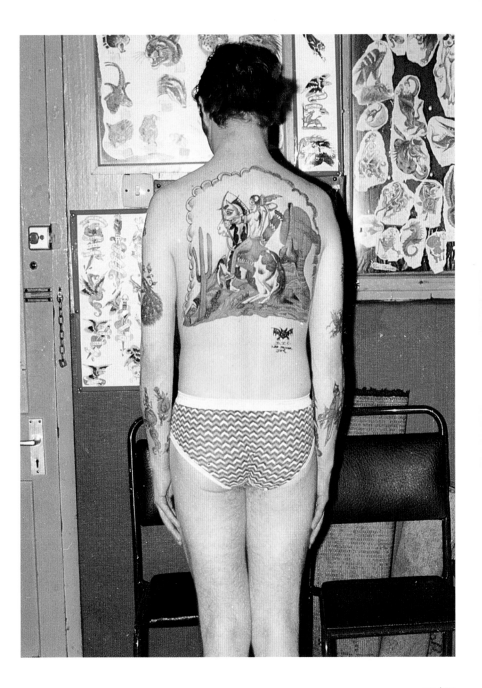

Artist Unknown, 1970s

Tattoo: Bill Skuse, Aldershot, Great Britain, 1960s

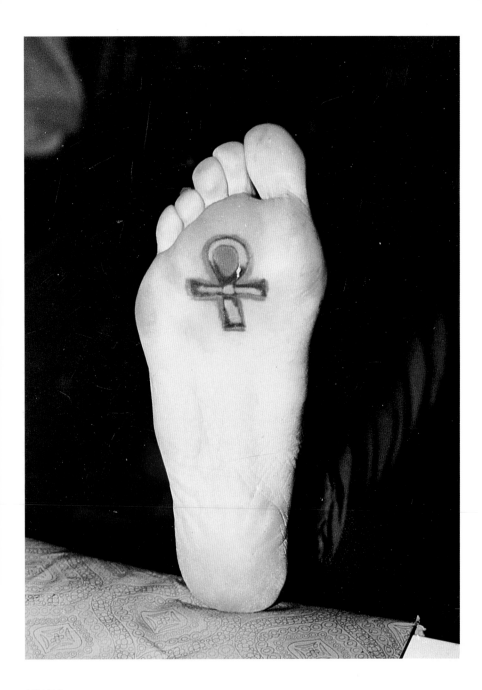

Artist Unknown, 1970s

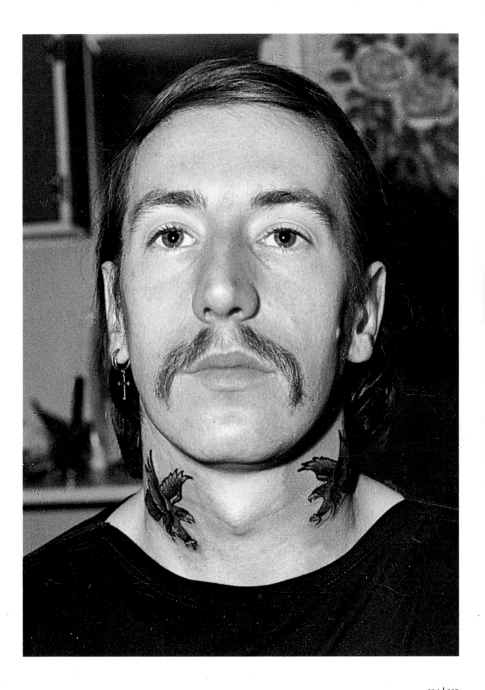

Artist Unknown, 1970s

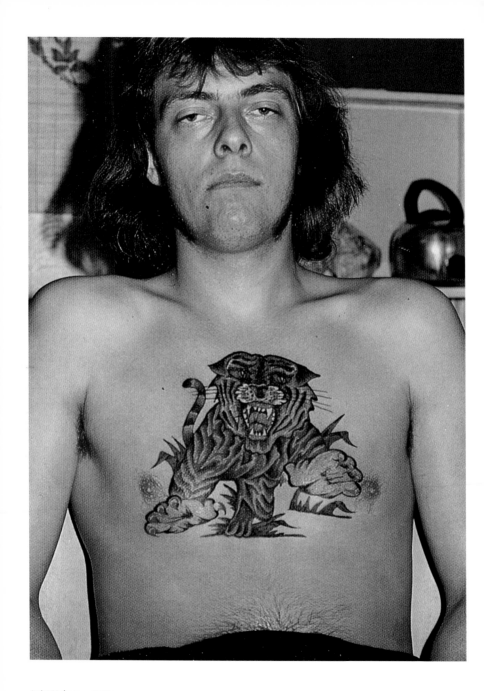

Artist Unknown, 1970s

Artist Unknown, France, 1970s

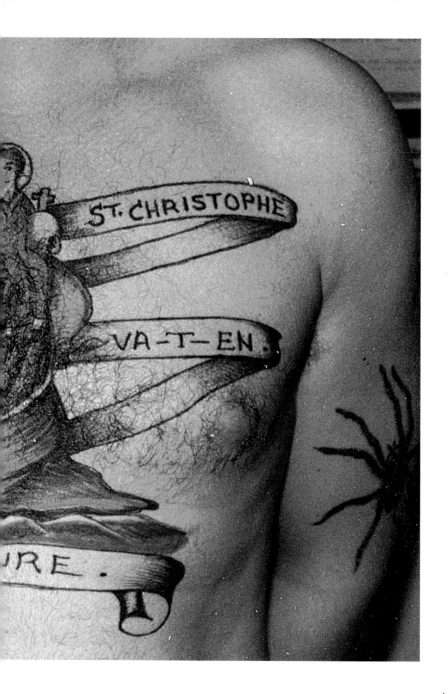

ST. CHRISTOPHE

VA-T-EN.

IRE.

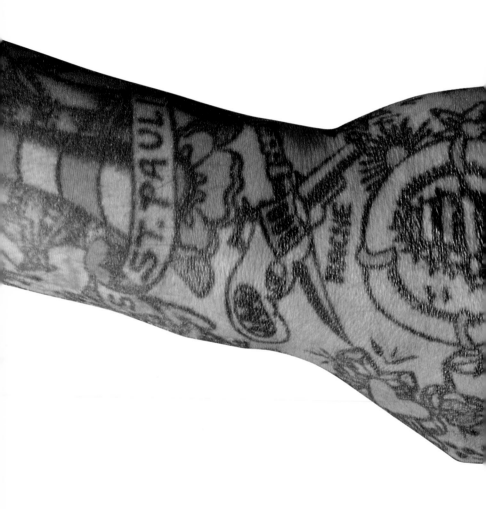

Herbert Krüger, Hamburg, Germany, 1974, Photo: Herbert Hoffmann

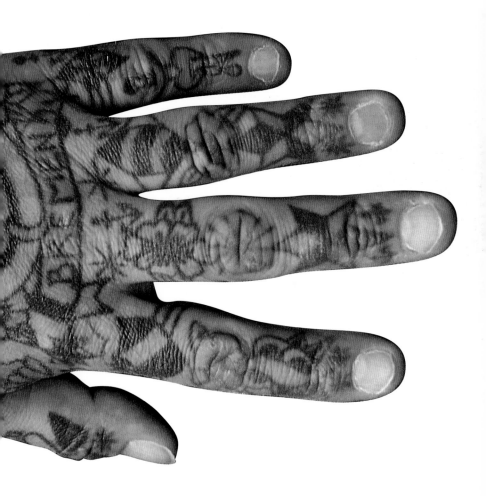

Artist Unknown, 1970s

Tattoo: Bob Maddison, Darlington, Great Britain, 1970s

Artist Unknown, 1970s

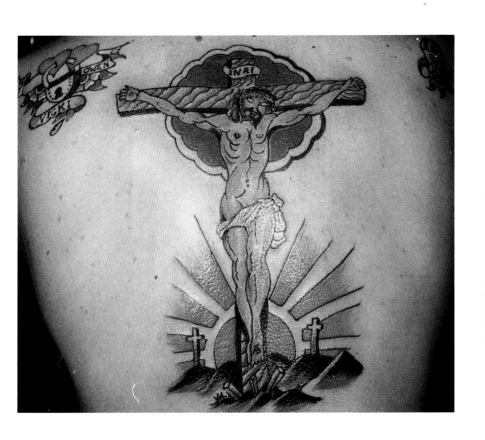

Tattoo: Bill Skuse, Aldershot, Great Britain, 1960s

Tattoo: George Bone, London, Great Britain, 1970s

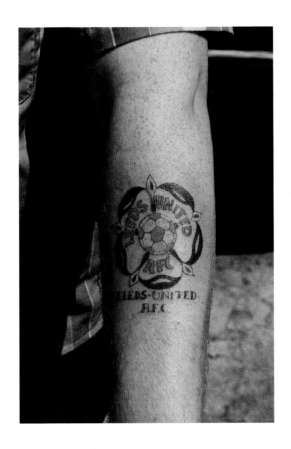

Artist Unknown, 1970s

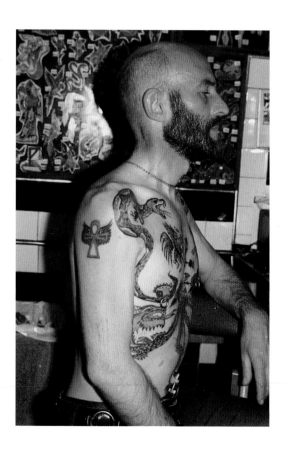

Artist Unknown, Great Britain, 1970s

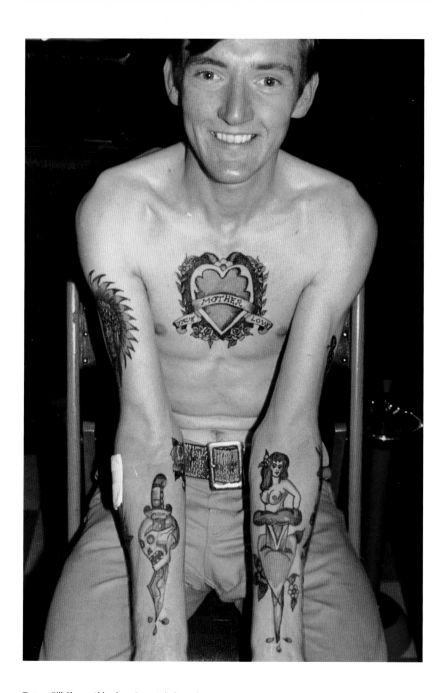

Tattoo: Bill Skuse, Aldershot, Great Britain, 1960s

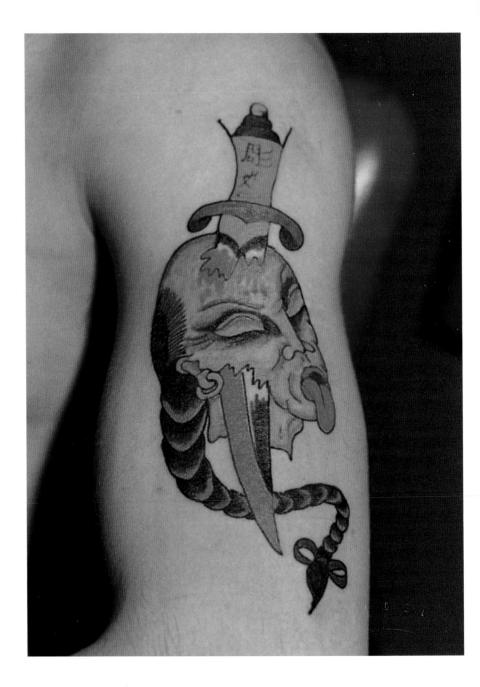

Tattoo: George Bone, London, Great Britain, 1970s

Artist Unknown, 1970s

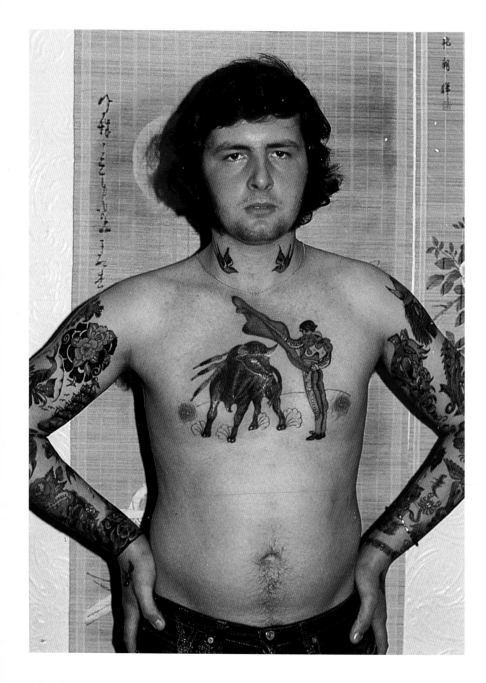

Artist Unknown, 1970s

Tattoo: Dean Dennis, San Francisco, USA (California), 1960s

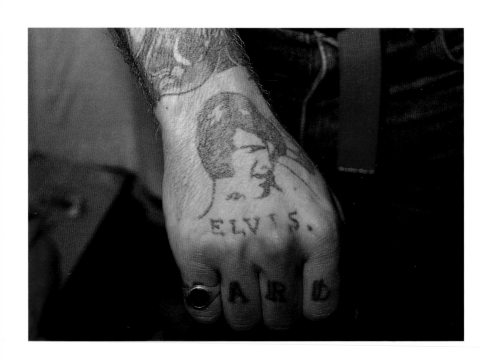

Artist Unknown, 1970s

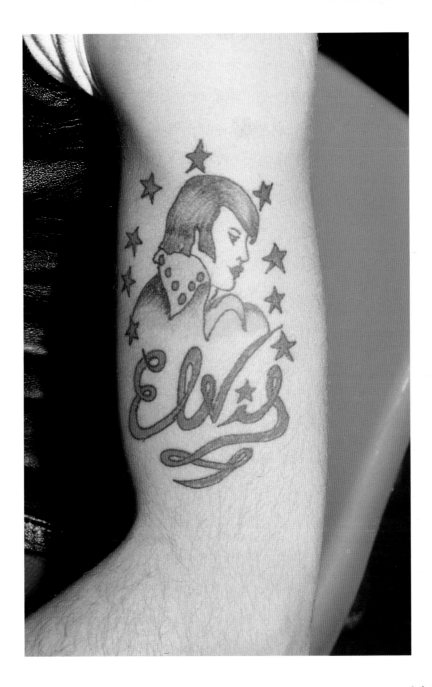

Tattoo: Artist Mosko David, Israel, with Swedish U.N. Soldiers, 1981

Histoire et Technique du Tatouage

En tant qu'expression artistique, le tatouage est aussi éphémère que la vie humaine. Il disparaît avec celui ou celle qui le porte. Les peintures rupestres, les sculptures et les monuments sont par essence beaucoup plus durables et peuvent témoigner de la culture des civilisations disparues. Pourtant, les tatouages sont des récits qui s'inscrivent eux aussi dans l'histoire de l'art. Mais ils sont mal acceptés ou mal perçus. Sauf bien sûr quand on les découvre sur des momies ou à travers des témoignages historiques – ceux d'Hérodote, de Marco Polo et, plus près de nous, de James Cook.

Le tatouage provoque les réactions les plus diverses – intérêt, étonnement, admiration, respect, gêne, répulsion. Le tatoué suscite un élan de sympathie chez les uns, des froncements de sourcils chez les autres. On l'envie ou on a peur de lui. Que l'on soit ignorant ou cultivé, large ou étroit d'esprit, que l'on aime ou non ce marquage du corps, le tatouage laisse toujours perplexe. Et l'on s'interroge moins sur ses aspects techniques que sur son sens et sa finalité. Or, cet aspect du phénomène est en général mal ou insuffisamment traité. Certes, il existe toute une littérature ethnographique sur le tatouage tel qu'il est pratiqué par de lointaines peuplades «primitives», mais les études se concentrent sur certains aspects du phénomène et non sur ce qui fait sa singularité. Cette lacune s'explique bien sûr par la complexité du sujet, et par le fait que le tatouage a toujours existé, qu'il est universel et qu'il est pratiqué pour toutes sortes de raisons. Comme le faisait déjà remarquer Darwin, il n'existe sur cette planète aucun peuple qui ne connaisse cette pratique.

La technique du tatouage n'a guère évolué au cours des siècles : elle consiste en gros à introduire des pigments sous la peau. En revanche, on note des différences de qualité qui dépendent du stade de développement et de l'inventivité des sociétés humaines. Ces différences tiennent à la maniabilité des outils d'une part et au souci esthétique de l'autre : le tatouage doit être finement tracé, et les lignes doivent être minces, noires et régulières. A cela s'ajoute le savoir-faire : appliquer la bonne quantité de pigments, pénétrer la peau suffisamment mais pas trop pour éviter de laisser des cicatrices, d'abîmer un muscle, de toucher une veine ou d'abîmer un os. Certaines populations « primitives » ont mis au point des techniques étonnantes pour tatouer les joues ou l'abdomen. C'est le cas des Inuits (qu'on appelait naguère « Esquimaux ») qui passent sous la peau, à l'aide d'une aiguille, un fil enduit de noir de fumée, brodant pour ainsi dire leurs tatouages au point par point. Cependant, ils ne cherchent pas à reproduire des modèles figuratifs, mais composent des motifs abstraits à partir de traits, pointillés, croix et lignes. Des surfaces importantes, comme le bras ou la cuisse, du genou à l'aine, ou encore le visage, peuvent être ainsi ornées de motifs géométriques.

On peut aussi inciser la peau de façon à délimiter des surfaces précises. Chaque compartiment est ensuite rempli de motifs représentant par exemple un lézard, ou encore des losanges, des cercles ou des étoiles. Une autre technique, moins précise, consiste à tracer des lignes et des courbes avec une pierre à bord tranchant. Certains peuples, comme les Thaïs, les Cambodgiens et les Birmans, grattent la peau avec un instrument muni d'une ou deux pointes effilées. Cette technique, qui permet de réaliser des tatouages complexes formés de nombreux points, spirales et autres figures, était déjà connue en Europe pendant la préhistoire et elle est toujours pratiquée par les Amérindiens (Indiens d'Amérique du Nord). Si elle ne se prête pas à la pigmentation intégrale de grandes surfaces, elle convient par contre très bien aux inscriptions calligraphiées caractéristiques de la tradition indochinoise. En Extrême-Orient, on se sert aussi d'une sorte de peigne formé d'un manche hérissé d'aiguilles ou de pointes d'os ou d'ivoire. Le tatoueur tient cet instrument d'une main et le frappe vivement avec un maillet qu'il tient dans l'autre main. Les pointes pénètrent ainsi dans la peau, que des assistants maintiennent tendue. Si elle est bien faite, cette opération est incroyablement rapide et efficace. On obtient ainsi de larges surfaces pigmentées et de grandes lignes continues. Les instruments utilisés mesurent jusqu'à cinq ou six centimètres de large. A Samoa, les tatoueurs réussissent à dessiner des surfaces et des lignes pigmentées particulièrement régulières. Des instruments plus petits et très effilés permettent de graver des motifs simples formés de lignes très fines, reproduits à quelques millimètres d'intervalle, et qui rappellent le tatouage facial moko des Maoris de Nouvelle-Zélande.

Une autre technique manuelle très répandue est celle qu'utilisent les Japonais (je passerai sous silence les procédés par le feu, avec ou sans pigment, par l'acide, la haute pression et le verre, qui donnent tous de médiocres résultats). Le tatoueur japonais se sert d'une série de baguettes à aiguilles réunies pour former un motif. Si les motifs simples n'exigent que trois aiguilles, il en faut plus pour tracer des lignes, et plus encore pour obtenir des surfaces noircies ou colorées : dans l'art du bokashi, il faut vingt-sept aiguilles pour obtenir les plus beaux dégradés du monde, allant du noir profond au gris le plus clair. Cependant, depuis l'invention de la machine à tatouer électrique, la méthode japonaise traditionnelle n'est plus pratiquée que dans les prisons par des tatoueurs chevronnés.

La machine à tatouer électrique, brevetée pour la première fois en 1891 par Samuel O'Reilly, n'a cessé depuis de se populariser. Produits en série, les accessoires et machines à tatouer représentent aujourd'hui un marché important. Depuis plus d'un siècle, on utilise toujours le principe d'entraînement à électro-aimant et ressort en spirale. Outre ces appareils à mouvement vertical, il existe aussi des machines à mouvement circulaire. Elles sont équipées d'une roue reliée à un moteur électrique. Une came transforme le mouvement circulaire en mouvement vertical. Si elles ont l'avantage d'être silencieuses, les machines à électro-aimant leur sont malgré tout bien supérieures. Les machines à mouvement circulaire se trouvent seulement chez les amateurs ou dans les prisons, où elles peuvent être raccordées à un magnétophone, un rasoir ou une brosse à dents électrique. Malgré tout, les résultats sont souvent étonnants.

Sur ces deux types de machines, l'aiguille est fixée à son support, par soudure pour le matériel professionnel, ou simplement maintenue avec de la ficelle, du mastic ou de la colle chez les amateurs. L'aiguille se déplace à l'intérieur d'un manche cylindrique, d'où elle sort pour piquer avant de se rétracter. Les manches professionnels sont réalisés en acier chirurgical, tandis que les amateurs peuvent aussi bien se servir de stylos que de douilles de cartouches, de pailles ou de cuillères recourbées, de supports en forme de L en bois, en plastique ou en aluminium, l'aiguille étant tenue avec de la mie de pain, du dentifrice, du chewing-gum, du goudron ou du plastique fondu, du fil de fer ou de la colle.

Les pigments utilisés proviennent du noir de fumée, de coques de noix brûlée, de résine, de cendres, ou encore de substances animales, végétales ou organiques mélangées à de l'alcool, de l'eau, de l'urine, de la salive, du sperme, du sang ou des sucs végétaux.

Les tatouages peuvent être exécutés lors de cérémonies ou de rites spéciaux, accompagnés de mantras, de chants ou de danses, et peuvent être aussi liés à une phase lunaire ou à une constellation spéciale, une saison, un deuil ou un événement heureux, une victoire ou une défaite. Le tatouage peut être le fruit d'une décision réfléchie.

Il peut aussi être subi sous la contrainte ou demandé dans un moment d'exaltation, parfois sous l'emprise de l'alcool ou de la drogue. Il se pratique dans un cadre traditionnel et religieux, mais aussi par sadisme ou superstition. On se fait tatouer pour une foule de raisons, dont beaucoup sont évoquées par Christopher Scott dans son passionnant (et très lisible) ouvrage, « Skin Deep Art, Sex and Symbols ».

La première raison mentionnée par Scott est le camouflage pour la chasse, dans le prolongement des peintures corporelles. Je ne connais aucun exemple concret de cette pratique. En revanche, l'existence de tatouages représentant des trophées ou des scènes de chasses fructueuses est attestée. Ils s'agirait dans ce cas de s'attirer la bienveillance des animaux ou de leur demander pardon. On trouve également des scènes de chasses cannibales représentant par exemple la décapitation d'un ennemi. A Bornéo, certains indigènes arborent fièrement sur la poitrine des tatouages qui font allusion à des rapts d'enfants et à leur mise en esclavage. Quant aux parents touchés par un tel drame, ils portent gravé sur la poitrine un motif stylisé, le « slengdang », qui symbolise le tissu servant à porter les enfants.

Le tatouage peut également avoir une fonction religieuse. Celui qui veut s'assurer une place au Ciel attire ainsi l'attention du dieu sur sa personne. Il signale de cette façon s'il est marié ou s'il attend toujours l'être qu'il va aimer. Les tatouages servent en quelque sorte de laissez-passer pour les différentes sphères de l'au-delà. Ils sont tellement importants qu'on les fait même sur les morts.

En Inde et au Tibet, les tatouages aident à traverser les périodes difficiles de la vie : puberté, maternité, maladie, deuil. La perte d'un proche est particulièrement propice au tatouage. On essaie de chasser un traumatisme affectif en se soumettant à des sévices physiques qui peuvent aller jusqu'à la mutilation, aux brûlures et à l'amputation (doigt écrasé ou coupé, cheveux arrachés, peau ou incisives arrachées, visage brûlé avec des pierres chauffées, etc.). C'est une façon de garder présent le souvenir d'un mort ou de l'honorer par un tatouage « in memoriam ». Les habitants de Hawaï exprimaient leur peine par des tatouages de deuil très particuliers : une série de points et de traits sur la langue. On devine que l'opération n'était pas exactement une partie de plaisir...

Le tatouage « memento mori » ou « in memoriam » est tout aussi répandu dans le monde occidental. Il perpétue généralement le souvenir de personnes respectées ou aimées, père, mère, frères ou sœurs. Il est souvent représenté par une croix, une rose et la mention du nom du défunt, mais il peut aussi prendre la forme d'un portrait ou d'une pierre tombale frappée d'une tête de mort. Ces expressions du deuil ne se limitent d'ailleurs pas à la perte d'êtres humains. C'est parfois ainsi qu'on pleure la mort d'un animal très aimé.

Les tatouages marquant les étapes de la vie (puberté, maternité ou crise de la quarantaine) sont d'une toute autre nature. Au moment de faire ses premiers pas dans le monde des adultes, l'adolescent pubère choisit des tatouages qui symbolisent son courage et son autonomie. En faisant ainsi graver ces signes sur sa peau, il s'associe à un groupe ou une sous-culture qu'il admire. De même certains quadragénaires expriment-ils à travers les tatouages une révolte et une individualité qui leur rappellent leur jeunesse.

Les tatouages de grossesse sont peu fréquents en Occident. Sous nos latitudes, rares sont les femmes qui acceptent de courir le risque d'une infection. En revanche, dans les cultures primitives, par l'intermédiaire de certains symboles, on tente d'influencer le sexe de l'enfant ou de s'assurer qu'il est sain ou qu'il n'est pas envoûté.

Dans de nombreuses régions du monde – et c'est là peut-être son aspect le plus connu –, le tatouage est un élément constitutif des rites d'initiation. Il représente le passage à un autre stade de la vie – du garçon à l'homme, de la fillette à la femme, de la femme à la mère – et marque du même coup les phases religieuses et sociales de l'existence. Tel un talisman, le tatouage protège des maladies, accidents et catastrophes, donnant force et fertilité. Cette croyance se manifeste à travers différents signes, ornements, symboles, contes et légendes, saints et héros. Ces tatouages sacrés sont également à l'origine du fameux « stop-bullet-tattoo » censé protéger de la mort par balle, et qui a soutenu la lutte héroïque du peuple karen pour son indépendance. Ces tatouages lui ont donné la force de braver l'armée birmane. On trouve des tatouages similaires dans l'armée thaïlandaise, ainsi que chez les Khmers rouges du Cambodge.

Pour être complet, signalons aussi l'existence de tatouages destinés à protéger contre des dangers plus anodins : morsures de chiens ou de serpents, mort par noyade et même accidents de la route. Certains tatouages sont également censés apporter richesse ou fécondité. Dans ce cas, ils sont exécutés lors d'une cérémonie rituelle, par un religieux ou un initié souvent généreusement rétribués.

Les tatouages jouent également un rôle vaccinal ou thérapeutique. Chez les Berbères et d'autres peuples, par exemple à Samoa, on peut se faire tatouer contre les rhumatismes. De l'Egypte à l'Afrique du Sud, on retrouve ces tatouages curatifs, fréquemment employés contre les affections oculaires et les maux de tête. Les Inuits et les Amérindiens se gravaient eux aussi sur la peau des signes destinés à les protéger des maladies. Les scarifications des jeunes filles noubas du Soudan ou dans d'autres pays d'Afrique, n'ont pas qu'une fonction esthétique. Elles sont aussi une forme traditionnelle de vaccin. En pratiquant de petites incisions, on renforce le système immunitaire et on réduit les risques d'infection lors des grossesses et des accouchements.

En Occident, les tatouages protecteurs existent sous d'autres formes. Pour se protéger de la noyade, les marins américains se tatouent un coq sur un pied et un cochon sur l'autre. Un portrait du Christ sur le dos protégeait jadis contre la flagellation : aucun capitaine, même le plus impitoyable, n'aurait osé frapper une image du Seigneur. Dans les Balkans, chez les Rom et les Sinti, les tatouages éloignaient les sorcières et le mauvais œil. Chez les pompiers d'Edo, l'actuel Tokyo, le motif du dragon protégeait contre les brûlures. Et les pêcheurs mélanésiens, se font encore volontiers tatouer des dauphins pour se protéger contre les requins.

Il existe donc mille façons de se prémunir du mal et d'adoucir la vie sur terre : en se conciliant les faveurs des démons de l'au-delà, avant et après le trépas, et en facilitant le passage de la vie à la mort, de la terre au paradis. Quant à ceux qui restent, ils ont aussi besoin de protection contre la mort.

On peut s'efforcer d'acquérir les qualités d'un ancêtre ou d'un esprit en s'en faisant tatouer la représentation symbolique sur la peau : le tatoueur choisit alors dans l'histoire du peuple ou de la tribu l'élément le plus favorable à son client, celui qui élèvera son rang social, l'incitera à la vertu, à la fierté, au respect du devoir. Le tatouage est un langage qui raconte des histoires d'héroïsme, de chasses fructueuses ou dangereuses, d'expéditions, de migrations, de propriétés, de dons, de courage et de force, d'invention et de persévérance. Sur les îles Mentawei, par exemple, on retrouve les lignes qui, sur les visages inuits, rappellent le souvenir d'un meurtre. Les spirales et les lignes tatouées sur les visages des Maoris évoquent clairement pour l'initié le passé et les qualités de celui qui les porte. Enfin, ces tatouages n'ont pas seulement une fonction terrestre. Ils jouent encore un rôle après la mort, notamment lors du passage devant le juge des âmes.

Le tatouage sert aussi à effrayer l'ennemi. Combien de fois n'ai-je pas tatoué des inscriptions et des symboles explosifs sur des gens qui n'auraient pas fait de mal à une mouche ! Je les ai vus s'évanouir à la vue d'une goutte de sang pendant que je gravais sur leur bras des inscriptions du genre « La mort plutôt que le déshonneur », « Tueur né » ou « J'emmerde le monde », ou des dessins de panthères noires, d'aigles aux ailes déployées ou de tigres en chasse. Pour impressionner un ennemi, il faut bien sûr des symboles forts. Poignard, tête de mort, panthère noire et autres disent clairement qu'il vaut mieux ne pas chercher la bagarre. Lors d'un combat, le tatouage peut détourner l'attention de l'adversaire et le déconcentrer quelques instants... un moment de distraction qui peut lui être fatal. Aux Iles Marquises, certains tatouages revêtent par exemple cette fonction. De grands yeux gravés sur la face intérieure du bras sont censés déstabiliser l'adversaire pendant quelques secondes. Il en va de même pour les tatouages faciaux mokos des Maoris, où les surfaces non tatouées rendent encore plus effrayants ces masques grimaçants destinés à faire fuir les adversaires ou à leur faire implorer grâce.

L'Occident connaît lui aussi ce genre de pratiques d'intimidation. Si la bagarre menace, il suffit qu'un tatoué retrousse ses manches pour que les choses s'apaisent... ou que le pugilat commence, selon le contexte. Lors des parties de « hanafuda », un jeu de cartes interdit par la police mais pratiqué illégalement dans des tripots, les gangters japonais, les yakusas, retirent leur kimono pour impressionner leurs adversaires avec leurs tatouages. Mike Tyson joue les provocateurs avec son tatouage du « grand Timonier » Mao Tsé-Tung, père de tous les Chinois et nageur fort médiatisé, dont on murmure qu'il ne détestait pas violer les petites filles. Mickey Rourke en fait autant avec son tatouage de l'IRA. J'ai même tatoué le signe du Ku-Klux-Klan sur un GI noir américain stationné en Allemagne et qui voulait ainsi battre les racistes sur leur propre terrain et avoir la paix dans son régiment. L'armée, qui ne savait que penser de ce geste, le rendit prématurément à la vie civile, tout en continuant à lui verser sa solde. Dans les camps de prisonniers russes, les fameux goulags, où les tatouages étaient très répandus, nombre d'épaules arboraient des inscriptions du type : « Une Russie sans les Rouges » ou « Je remercie mes maîtres communistes pour cette jeunesse heureuse », agrémentées d'un dessin représentant un visage émacié d'enfant derrière des barbelés, sur fond de miradors et de projecteurs. Fréquents également, les tatouages sur l'abdomen : ils représentaient Lénine ou Staline sous forme de cochons marqués de croix gammées, crucifiés, forniquant avec un autre cochon, se livrant à une fellation sur le diable ou fumant de l'opium. Ces actes de provocation ne pouvaient être effacés que par traitement à l'acide ou élimination pure et simple du tatoué. Le tatouage constitue dans ce cas une forme extrême de contestation. Il donne la force de survivre, de s'affirmer face aux humiliations quotidiennes.

Le tatouage peut également servir de parure érotique et stimuler l'excitation en rendant le corps plus attrayant sexuellement. C'est la fonction que lui assignent les amateurs de cuir ou de latex, les adeptes du piercing et des rapports sado-maso. A l'inverse, les tatouages peuvent aussi inviter à la douceur et à la tendresse. Certains ont une signification spécifiquement érotique : lesbiennes en position 69, jolie créature montrant ses fesses, langue des Rolling Stones, allusions au phallus ou à l'érection et dessins sur le bas-ventre ou les reins constituent autant d'invites à l'acte sexuel. Inscriptions ou symboles signalent à un éventuel partenaire les préférences sexuelles du tatoué.

Les tatouages peuvent également délivrer des messages d'amour ou d'amitié, des formules patriotiques ou de révolte. Les exemples ne manquent pas : « Made in England » ou « Germany » pour les skinheads nationalistes; « Mutter », « mom » et « maman » pour des fervents de la famille. Les allusions à des aventures amoureuses ne sont pas rares : « Celle que j'aime est la femme d'un autre », « A Ginette pour la vie, « amour toujours » ou tout simplement le nom de l'être aimé. L'anarchisme et la révolte s'expriment souvent à travers des symboles violents où dominent le meurtre, la guerre, le racisme, la drogue et les perversions sexuelles. Il ne faut pas toujours prendre trop littéralement ces provocations, qui traduisent souvent davantage le désespoir, la frustration et le sentiment d'humiliation du tatoué que ses véritables intentions. Une jeune femme juive m'a un jour demandé d'effacer une croix gammée qu'elle portait sur la main. Ce symbole, qu'elle s'était fait étourdiment tatouer en Inde, avait été très mal accueilli par ses proches quand elle était rentrée chez elle (il faut préciser qu'avant que les nazis ne se l'approprient, la svastika symbolisait la santé, la joie et le dynamisme du cosmos). Parmi les signes les plus connus, citons les trois points tatoués, entre le pouce et l'index. Ils signifient « Mort aux vaches » (en clair : aux policiers). Ils ne valent certainement pas un traitement de faveur dans les commissariats... Les tatouages peuvent aussi marquer certains événements personnels : mariage, décès, anniversaire ou autres dates, lieux, bons ou mauvais souvenirs. Les pèlerins – coptes, arméniens, musulmans, chrétiens, bouddhistes ou hindouistes –, se faisaient tatouer à l'occasion du pèlerinage, que ce soit à Jérusalem, la Mecque ou Saint-Jacques-de-Compostelle. Quant aux marins, ces hommes sans foi ni loi, ils arborent l'image de « leur » port ou illustrent le passage de l'équateur, du Cap Horn ou du Cap de Bonne-Espérance. Les soldats, eux, se font tatouer le nom des batailles et des victoires auxquelles ils ont participé, comme Saigon pour les anciens combattants du Vietnam. On retiendra comme élément commun à tous ces exemples l'affirmation de l'identité du tatoué.

Le tatouage peut aussi signer l'appartenance à un groupe. En arborant tel symbole, on indique que l'on fait ou que l'on aimerait faire partie de tel groupe. Dans ce domaine aussi, les exemples ne manquent pas. Chez les peuples primitifs, on porte le signe de sa tribu, le totem, un signe connu de tous ou au contraire tenu secret, comme les signes magiques de la société secrète Kakean, qui rassemblait les chasseurs de têtes sur l'île Céram, dans l'archipel indonésien. Les scarifications des Yorubas du Nigéria indiquent également l'appartenance à un clan, de même que les tatouages des Hells Angels ou des bandes de rue des grandes villes américaines, les signes tatoués des triades chinoises ou les divers signes de reconnaissance des groupes de rock'n roll. Tous indiquent ou suggèrent l'appartenance à un groupe, à un milieu ou à un mode de vie.

Autrefois, pour gagner leur vie, certains artistes de cirque se faisaient tatouer le corps, mais cette pratique s'est perdue de nos jours. Il n'existe plus que quelques cas isolés, comme par exemple « Enigma », l'homme-puzzle du Jim Rose Circus Side Show, dont le corps est entièrement recouvert d'un motif de puzzle. « Great Omi » et l'homme-zèbre figurent aussi parmi les plus célèbres tatoués « intégraux ». Les tatoués étaient de grandes attractions dans les cirques et les foires, et ils gagnaient très bien leur vie, surtout aux Etats-Unis. Chez les dames, citons Betty Broadbent et la Belle Irene. Mentionnons aussi le couple Frank et Anni van den Burg. Aux Etats-Unis, il existait même une famille où le fils et la fille portaient les mêmes tatouages que leurs parents. Mais le sommet du genre était la vache tatouée qui tirait une charrette pleine d'enfants à Coney Island.

D'autres tatouages peuvent rapporter de l'argent d'un coup, par exemple à la suite d'un défi du style : « Je parie que tu ne te feras pas tatouer des lunettes sur le visage. » En 1975, à Amsterdam, j'ai rencontré un Belge qui avait effectivement gagné un tel pari. Le médecin de la prison avait eu beau intervenir, on en devinait encore les contours comme taillés au couteau sur sa peau grêlée.

Les tatouages de marques ou de logos d'entreprises qui apparaissent aujourd'hui fréquemment dans la publicité sont en général simplement peints sur la peau le temps de prendre la photo. Mais on peut aussi engager quelqu'un qui a déjà le tatouage désiré. En effet, il n'est pas rare que des fans se fassent tatouer leur marque préférée : Harley Davidson est bien sûr très prisée, ainsi que Jack Daniels, Gauloise, Lucky Strike, Chanel, Durex, Heineken, Nike, Mercedes, Cadillac, Thunderbird, Ferrari, Jaguar et même Rolls Royce. Parmi les grands classiques, citons aussi les crocodiles Lacoste tatoués sur la poitrine et la marque Wrangler sur la fesse droite. Je porte moi-même un film Kodachrome, hommage à la meilleure pellicule du monde, mais cela ne m'a jamais rapporté un sou !

Certains tatouages servent en outre à donner des indications médicales, comme le groupe sanguin, que les soldats SS se faisaient tatouer sur l'avant-bras. Cette pratique est encore en vigueur dans les armées américaine et anglaise, ainsi qu'aux légions étrangères française et espagnole. On peut néanmoins déplorer qu'il n'existe aucun règlement précisant où se faire tatouer. Cela éviterait au médecin d'avoir à ausculter tout le corps quand le patient est inanimé. Pour ma part, j'ai proposé de faire tatouer les donneurs d'organes à l'encre invisible, en un endroit convenu, de façon à ce qu'un médecin puisse reconnaître rapidement le tatouage à la lumière noire. Cela ferait gagner un temps précieux, les accidentés ayant rarement sur eux leur certificat de donneur. Lors des séances de rayons, des tatouages servent également à repérer les parties cancéreuses.

La proposition tout à fait fasciste de marquer les porteurs du virus HIV est particulièrement choquante. De nos jours, le tatouage ne sert plus à châtier ni à marquer les esclaves, les voleurs ou les violeurs. Dans ce domaine, l'exemple le plus atroce est celui de l'Holocauste. Etant bien informés sur les traditions juives, les nazis savaient que la loi de Moïse interdisait aux juifs de se tatouer. Ainsi, les tatouages qu'ils pratiquaient n'avaient pas qu'une fonction réglementaire, mais contribuaient à humilier les prisonniers des camps, de même qu'on les rasait, qu'on leur arrachait les dents, qu'on désinfectait leurs vêtements, qu'on leur faisait porter l'étoile jaune, la marque des Tsiganes, le triangle rose des homosexuels, le signe des communistes et un numéro matricule, marqué sur la veste et tatoué sur la peau des enfants, des vieillards, des hommes et des femmes.

En Indochine, les tatouages servaient autrefois à recenser le peuple. En Thaïlande, celui qui falsifiait les données d'un tel tatouage risquait l'extermination totale de sa famille. Dans les zoos, les laboratoires et instituts de recherche, il n'est pas rare de tatouer les animaux. Dans ce cas, chiens, chevaux, poules ou lapins sont marqués pour des raisons administratives.

Enfin, les tatouages peuvent relayer les produits de beauté et servir à dissimuler des taches ou à graver des maquillages : eye-liner, grains de beauté ou rouge à lèvres. J'ai également rencontré un Belge qui s'était fait tatouer des poils sur la poitrine et de la barbe sur les joues. On peut aussi se faire tatouer une aréole après ablation partielle d'un sein, ou dissimuler une cicatrice avec un tatouage de la couleur de la peau. J'ai discuté un jour avec un Blanc qui voulait devenir noir en se tatouant de la tête aux pieds. Vaste programme...

Les tatouages des détenus ont déjà été mentionnés à propos du goulag et des bandes. L'inscription « Coupez ici » accompagnée de pointillés tatoués sur le cou ironise sur la fonction du bourreau. En dépit de leur interdiction et de règlements prévoyant souvent de lourdes peines disciplinaires, les tatouages sont très fréquents dans le milieu pénitentiaire. Ils traduisent une révolte contre la déshumanisation. C'est le signe que le détenu ne se laisse pas aller, qu'il n'est pas vaincu. C'est la preuve que l'esprit est libre, même si le corps est prisonnier. Les tatouages racontent sur le mode de la dérision le temps passé en prison. C'est le cas des prisonniers russes qui figurent les années de prison par des clochetons d'églises. Le délit, la peine infligée et les rapports de force dans le camp ou la prison peuvent également apparaître clairement sur les doigts. « Fraternité aryenne », « White Power », croix gammées, « 100 % Blanc », « K.K.K. » sont autant de tatouages répandus parmi les Blancs américains pour indiquer l'union des prisonniers blancs contre l'ennemi noir. Quant aux tatouages de bandes, les plus connus sont « mi vida loca » (« ma vie de fou »), les trois points des Chicanos des Etats-Unis, le Zigizigi Sputnik et la Bahala. Toutes ces bandes sont composées d'individus qui partagent les mêmes conditions de vie misérables. Aux Philippines, à Manille, où la quasi-totalité des prisonniers porte un signe d'appartenance à une bande, la police appréhende les gens dans la rue à la simple vue d'un tatouage.

La pratique du tatouage dépend du niveau économique et culturel d'une société. En effet, le raffinement culturel n'est possible que lorsqu'un peuple est sédentarisé et qu'il se consacre à l'agriculture. La pensée mythique et spirituelle peut alors s'enrichir, et différentes formes artistiques peuvent s'épanouir. Bien qu'ils ne transmettent pas leur histoire par l'écrit, mais par l'oral, beaucoup de peuples soi-disant primitifs peuvent remonter à 90 ou 100 générations. Cette transmission du passé repose aussi bien sur la parure corporelle que sur la sculpture, le dessin, le tissage ou l'architecture. Ainsi, une corde passée plusieurs fois autour d'une poutre peut indiquer le nombre d'embarcations qui ont permis la migration d'un peuple. A Samoa, le triangle tatoué au niveau des reins, sous la ceinture du pantalon, renvoie au « chien volant », la chauve-souris, et marque l'endroit où se situe la tache mongolique, une coloration bleue de la peau, caractéristique des habitants de cette région d'Asie, et qui est visible pendant six jours après la naissance avant de s'estomper. Ces indications attestant l'origine d'un peuple sont très importantes. Ne disposant que de peu de biens et d'outils, les peuples nomades ne pratiquent guère le tatouage, ou alors sous une forme rudimentaire. Au cours de l'histoire de l'humanité, les peuples qui ont produit les plus belles œuvres d'art sont ceux qui construisaient des maisons, pratiquaient l'agriculture, connaissaient leur passé, vivaient au sein de structures hiérarchisées. C'étaient souvent des chasseurs de têtes belliqueux et redoutés. Les tatouages jouaient un rôle important dans la vie du groupe, tant du point de vue hiérarchique que religieux, social, guerrier ou héroïque. Pour être digne de respect, il faut supporter, sans gémir ni montrer de signe de faiblesse, des opérations douloureuses comme le tatouage, le piercing, la brûlure, l'amputation ou le jeûne. «Apprends à souffrir sans te plaindre», telle est la devise gravée sur la poitrine du plus célèbre amateur allemand de tatouages, le Hambourgeois Theo Vetter. Cependant, une population qui lutte quotidiennement pour sa survie et assure avec peine sa subsistance n'a guère le temps ni l'envie de sacrifier à des préoccupations artistiques. En revanche, les peuples qui ont produit des chefs-d'œuvre artistiques pratiquaient tous le tatouage : Bataks, Toradjas, Nagas, Ibans, Kayans, Igorots, Ifugaos et Kalingas, les premiers vivant en Indonésie, principalement à Bornéo, et les trois derniers dans le Nord des Philippines. Dans la région Pacifique, l'art est également le fait de peuples «tatoueurs». En Nouvelle-Zélande, les Maoris ont porté l'art du tatouage jusqu'à la perfection. Le marquage du corps n'est donc en rien un signe de barbarie, mais témoigne au contraire d'une civilisation très évoluée.

Dans le monde industrialisé, le tatouage est généralement pratiqué par les plus défavorisés – délinquants, marins, prostituées, soldats, aventuriers et détraqués d'une part, ou à l'inverse par les excentriques de la haute société, membres de la noblesse, intellectuels ou artistes en quête de nouveauté. Au début du siècle, les tatouages étaient très répandus dans l'élite : les maisons princières, le tsar et la tsarine, les familles américaines les plus riches, les Fürstenburg, Vanderbilt, l'empereur Guillaume II et même Lady Churchill. Il en va de même pour les célébrités d'aujourd'hui : les vedettes du cinéma, les chanteurs de rock et d'innombrables artistes portent des tatouages. Ce sont des modèles, des représentants de la culture qui agissent sur la mode. Par leur image et leur comportement, des gens comme Mickey Rourke, Sean Connery, Sean Penn, Dennis Hopper, Whoopi Goldberg, Roseanne Barr, Johnny Depp, Drew Barrymore, Julia Roberts,

David Bowie, Axel Rose, Lenny Kravitz, les Red Hot Chili Peppers, Pearl Jam, Cypress Hill, Green Day, les Beastie Boys, Nirvana ou les Smashing Pumpkins influencent la vie, l'art, la mode, la morale, la démocratie, l'émancipation et la façon de penser de la société tout entière. Tous portent des tatouages, dont certains exécutés par mes soins. Les tatouages, symboles d'hier et d'aujourd'hui, font fureur dans les vidéoclips. Le motif de la côte nord-ouest, principalement diffusé par Dave Shore et John Hullenaar dit « The Dutchman », provient en fait de tribus amérindiennes de cette région – Tlingits, Haïdas ou Kwakiutls. Ce motif doit entre autres sa célébrité au tatouage dorsal que j'ai réalisé pour Anthony Kiedis, le chanteur des Red Hot Chili Peppers. Pour populariser un tatouage, rien ne vaut le concours d'une star!

Les tatouages constituent un langage rapidement décodable. Cela se vérifie aussi bien dans les cultures dites primitives que dans notre monde réputé civilisé. Cependant, les tatouages sont beaucoup plus hermétiques en Occident pour les non-initiés que, par exemple, dans les peuplades dites primitives en général, et cela pour la simple raison qu'il existe chez nous des quantités phénoménales de motifs. Il n'empêche que tout le monde reconnaît les signes propres à certaines sous-cultures comme celles des punks, des skinheads ou des rockers.

Les symboles du rock sont particulièrement faciles à décoder: ils sont imposants, lourds, monochromes, à base de crânes et d'ailes, de marques de motos comme Harley Davidson et d'abréviations comme « F.T.W. » (« Fuck The World ») ou simplement « Fuck You » tatouées sur les doigts. Ces symboles datent des années 60 et ont été popularisés par les bikers américains qui ont fait de la moto un art de vivre, sillonnant les Etats-Unis tels des nomades. Les premiers clubs de motards choquèrent les gardiens de la morale, surtout les clubs qui avaient été fondés sur la côte ouest des Etats-Unis, comme les Galopping Gooses, les Pegans ou les Hells Angels. Après l'affaire Hollister, une histoire de viol jamais élucidée, les services dirigés par J. Ed Hoover firent tout pour marginaliser les clubs de motards. Il faut dire que, loin de se cacher, leurs membres arboraient fièrement sur leur dos les couleurs et insignes de leur club. Les conservateurs firent alors de la répression anti-motards un argument électoral. Ceux qui briguaient un poste de shérif, de commissaire, de maire, de sénateur ou de procureur organisaient, avec le concours des médias, des rafles spectaculaires. Les arrestations étaient assorties de cautions astronomiques. La plupart des individus appréhendés étaient relâchés après les élections sans qu'aucune charge ne soit retenue contre eux. Et si plus tard ils réclamaient et obtenaient des dommages et intérêts, c'était bien sûr les contribuables qui devaient payer.

A la suite de cette chasse aux sorcières, l'association des motards américains voulut se distancier de ses membres les plus voyants. Tous ceux qui portaient tatouages et veste en jean coupée furent donc exclus, mais ils ne représentaient guère qu'un pour cent des membres. Ils choisirent alors leurs propres signes distinctifs, qu'ils portaient fièrement tatoués : le chiffre « 13 », pour symboliser la treizième lettre de l'alphabet, le « M » de marijuana, en général accompagné de la devise « Live to Ride, Ride to Live » (vivre pour la moto, la moto pour vivre). Le mouvement eut un grand succès. Il publiait un magazine où les bikers parlaient de ce qui les intéresssait – et notamment du tatouage. Comprenant qu'il y avait là un créneau à prendre, les fabricants mirent sur le marché des appareils à tatouer. Les cabinets de tatouage se multiplièrent rapidement. Mais, faute d'information, en particulier sur la façon de disposer et de souder les aiguilles, la technique la plus courante devint celle à une seule aiguille, pratiquée à l'origine dans les prisons. La plupart des amateurs n'avaient aucune connaissance sur le tatouage traditionnel, et ils enrichirent – ou plutôt appauvrirent – le répertoire en tatouant des motifs absurdes, comme celui du château fort. Malgré quelques tatoueurs de talent, le style de ces amateurs était condamné à disparaître. Aujourd'hui, les tatoueurs professionnels sont plus nombreux. Le public est mieux informé, attaché à la qualité et au conseil de spécialistes. Certains dessinateurs particulièrement doués ont fait carrière dans le domaine du tatouage, comme Bob Roberts, Mike Malone, Jack Rudy et Dave Shore. Mais il faut surtout citer Ed Hardy, formé auprès de grands maîtres du tatouage traditionnel comme Zeke Owen et Sailor Jerry Collins de Honolulu, et plus tard Horihide Kazuo Oguri de Gifu au

Japon, qui devint l'un des plus grands tatoueurs de tous les temps. Hardy a enrichi l'art du tatouage de motifs ethniques traditionnels, ceux des Ibans et des Dayaks de Bornéo par exemple. Il écrit également. Son livre « Tattoo Time » est devenu légendaire, et « Modern Primitives », tiré à 120000 exemplaires, a ouvert la voie à la mode actuelle du piercing.

Les photos de ce livre proviennent presque toutes des archives de l'« Amsterdam Tattoo Museum ».

Le musée et sa bibliothèque, inaugurés en mai 1996, sont les seuls consacrés à l'histoire du tatouage. L'essentiel du fonds se compose des collections Skuse und Kobel, que j'ai eu la chance d'acquérir, comme j'ai pu en vingt ans acheter maintes autres successions et collections de photos : des cartons entiers de négatifs, de tirages originaux, de copies et bien sûr, de catalogues de tatouages, le tout représentant un demi-siècle d'histoire.

En règle générale, le prix de chaque cliché est fixe. Cependant, le prix des tirages de la collection Skuse est fonction de la présence ou non d'organes génitaux. La plupart des photos de cet ouvrage ont été prises par des anonymes, le plus souvent les tatoueurs eux-mêmes. J'aimerais les remercier ici, ainsi que leurs modèles. Sans eux, ce livre n'aurait jamais pu voir le jour.

Henk Schiffmacher

The Amsterdam Tattoo Museum, The Netherlands, 1996

Japanese Tattoos

Tattoos: Horiyoshi III, Yokohama

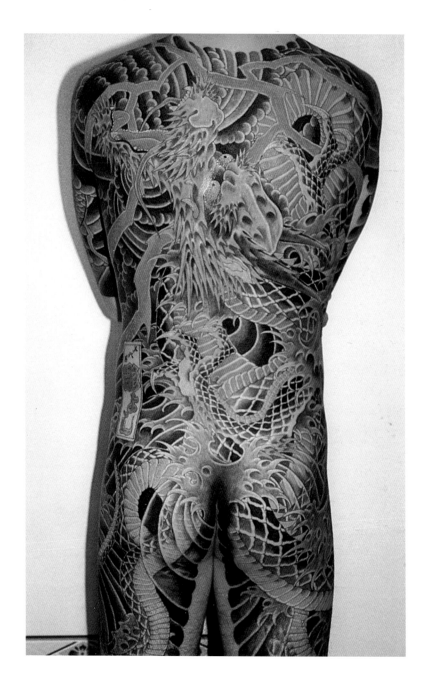

Artist Unknown

Mitsuaki Ohwada at Work, Yokohama

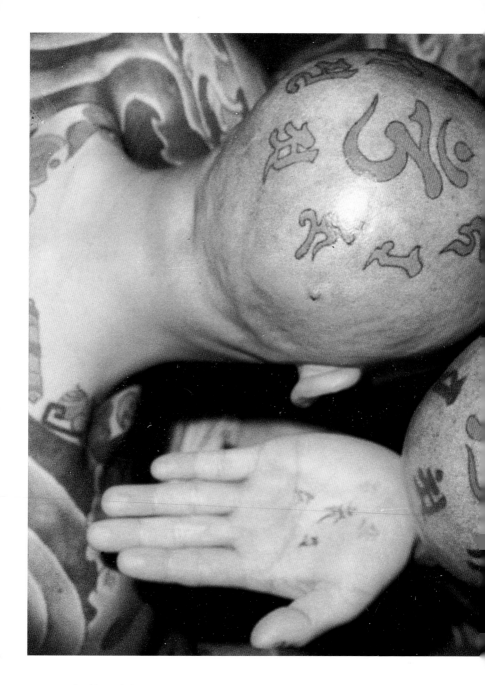

Tattoos: Horiyoshi III, Yokohama

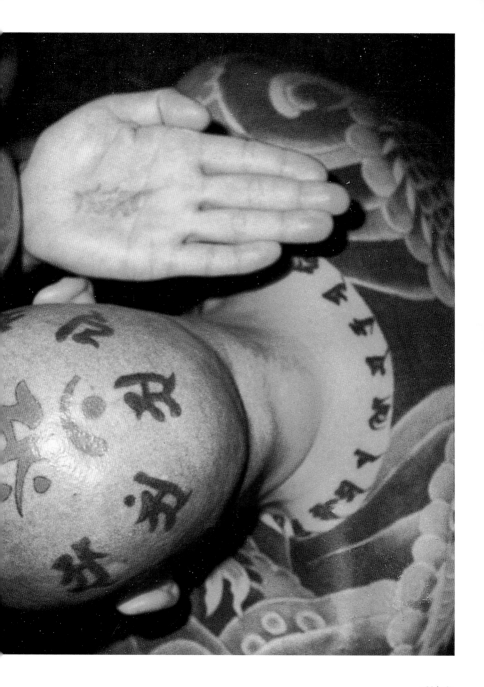

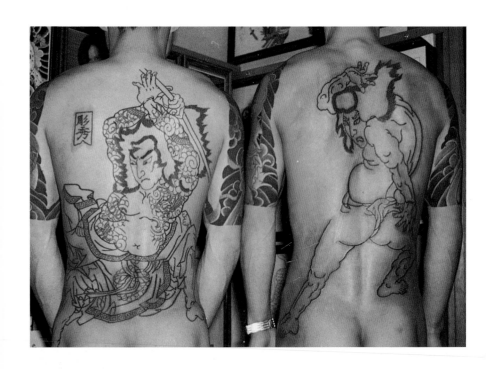

Tattoos: Kazuo Oguri, Gifu City (unfinished)

Tattoo Design: Kazuo Oguri, Gifu City

Tattoo Club of Japan, Yokohama

Tattoo: Horiyoshi, Yokohama

Mitsuaki Ohwada in his Studio, Yokohama

Unknown Tattoo Artist at Work

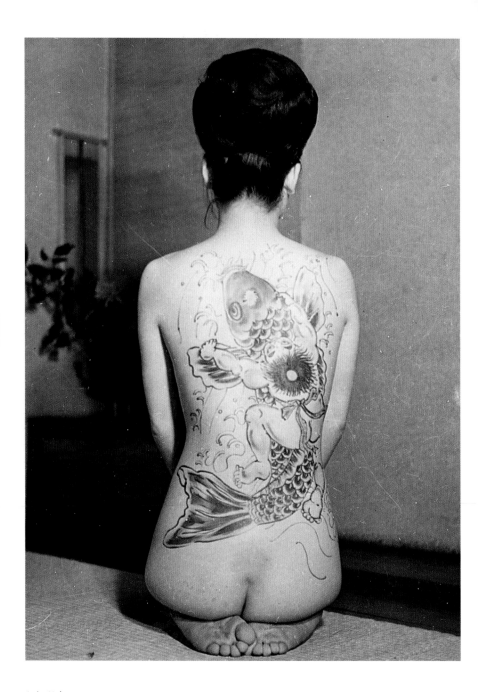

Artist Unknown

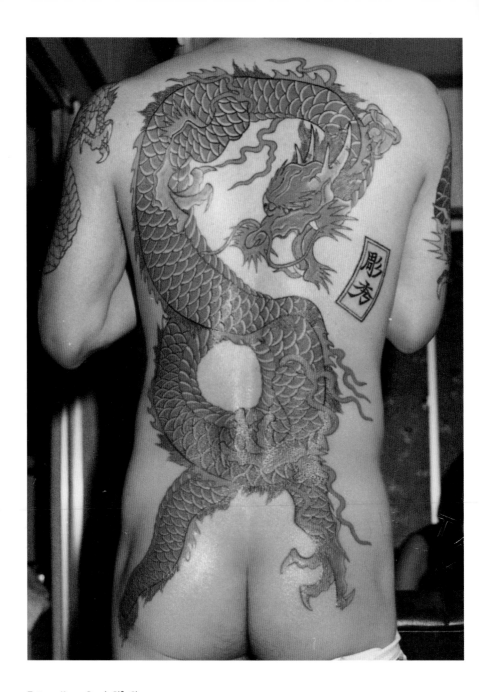

Tattoos: Kazuo Oguri, Gifu City

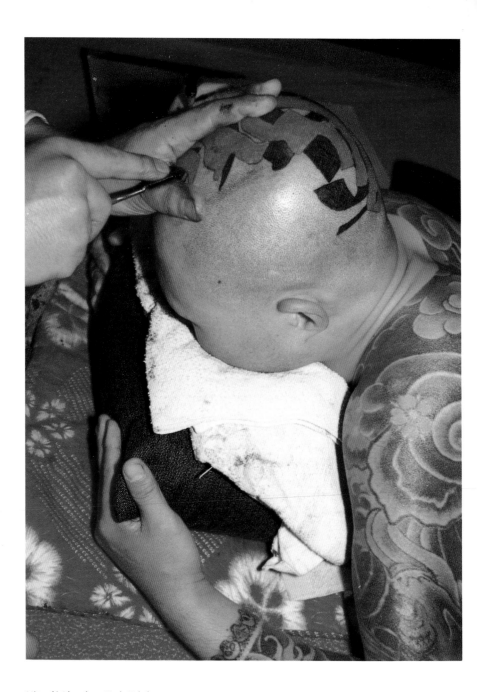

Mitsuaki Ohwada at Work, Yokohama

Artist Unknown

Tattooing Process

Tattoo: Mitsuaki Ohwada, Yokohama

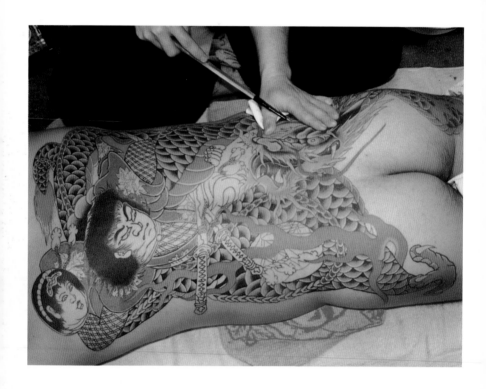

Tattoo: Horiwaka, Tokyo

Tattoo: Horiwaka, Tokyo

Tattoo: Kazuo Oguri, Gifu City (tattoo in progress)

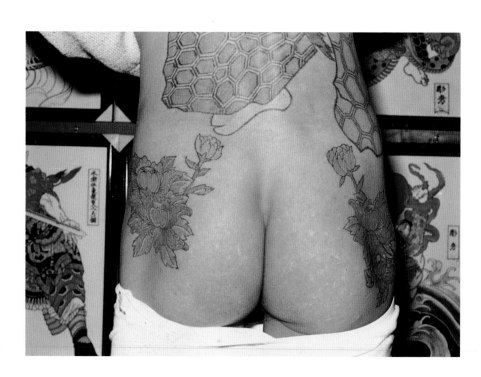

Tattoos: Kazuo Oguri, Gifu City

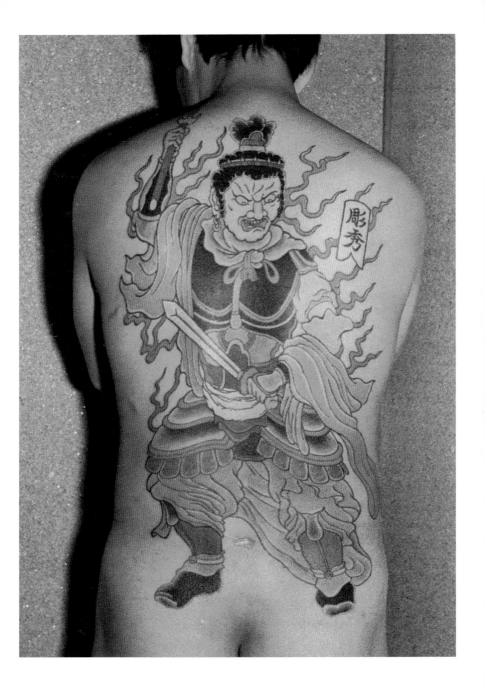

Tattoos: Kazuo Oguri, Gifu City (two different stages)

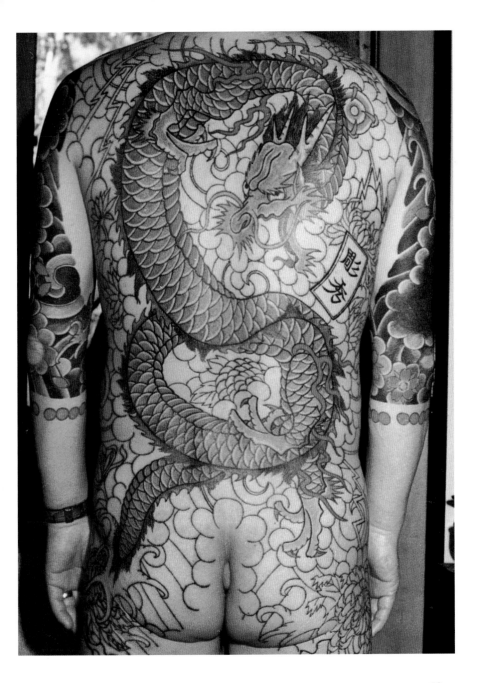

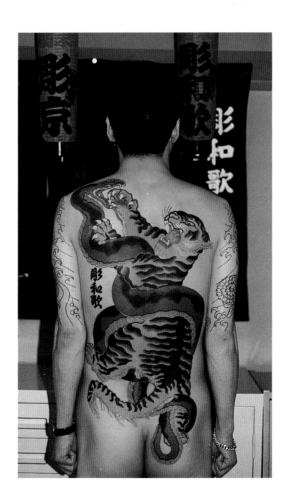

Tattoo: Horiwaka, Tokyo

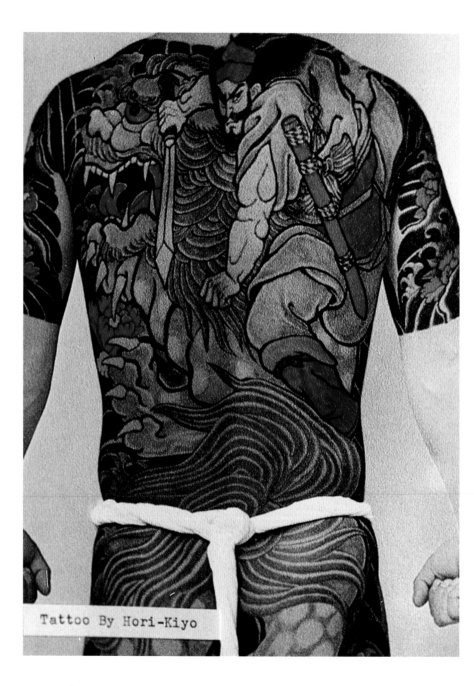

Tattoos: Hori-Kyo

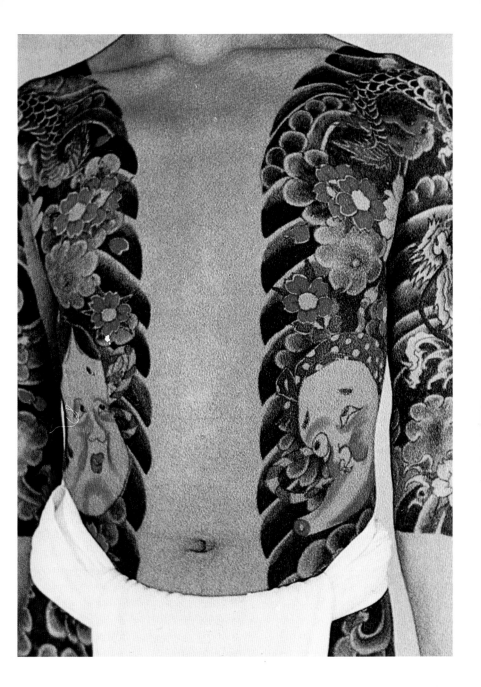

Tattoo Design: Kazuo Oguri, Gifu City

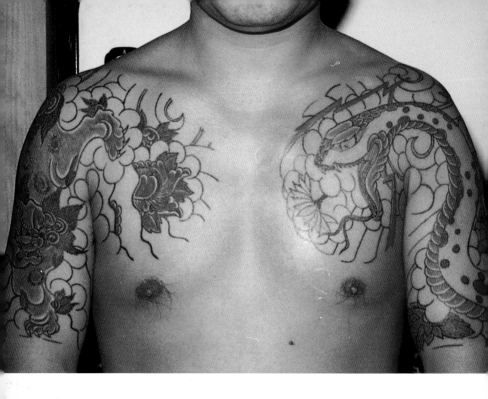

Tattoos: Kazuo Oguri, Gifu City (left tattoo in progress)

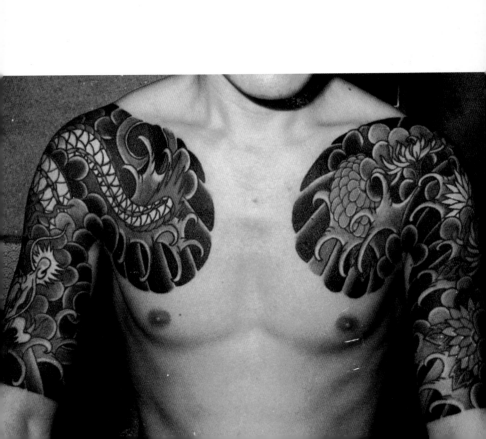

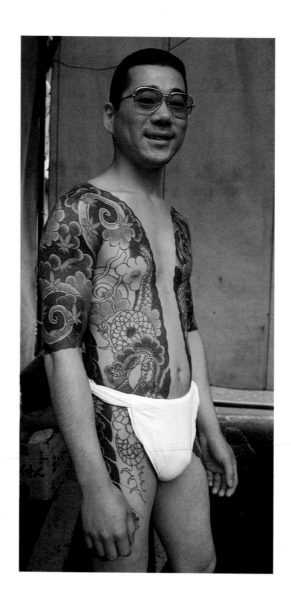

Artist Unknown

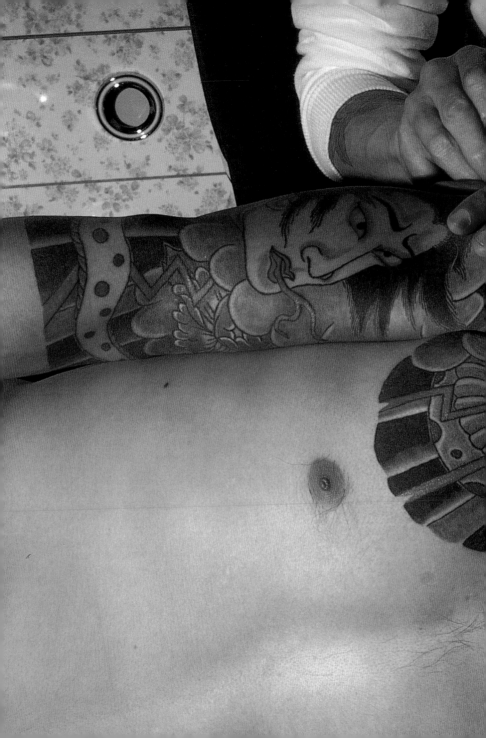

Tattoos: Kazuo Oguri, Gifu City (tattoos in progress)

Tattoos: Kazuo Oguri, Gifu City (two different stages)

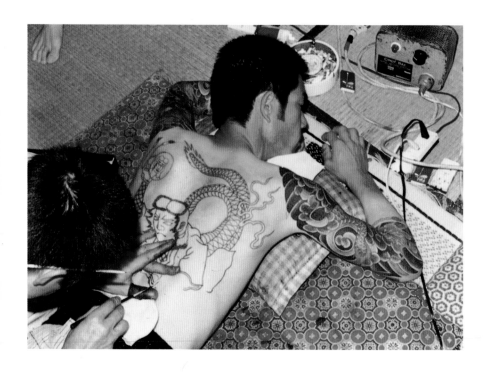

Kazuo Oguri at Work, Gifu City

Tattoos: Kazuo Oguri, Gifu City (left tattoo in progress)

Tattoos: Horiyoshi III, Yokohama

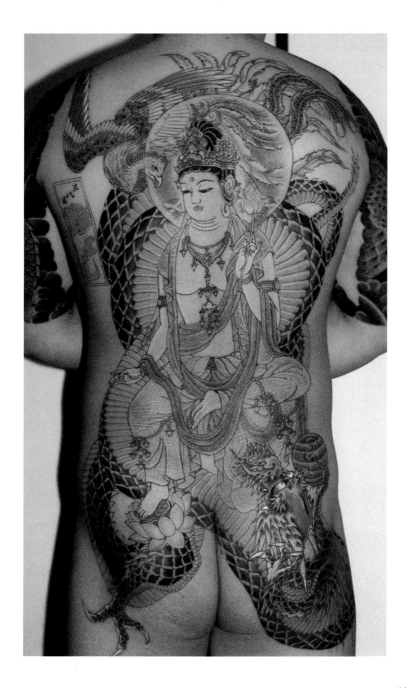

Contemporary Tattoo Art

Tattoo: Dave Lum, Salem, USA (Oregon)

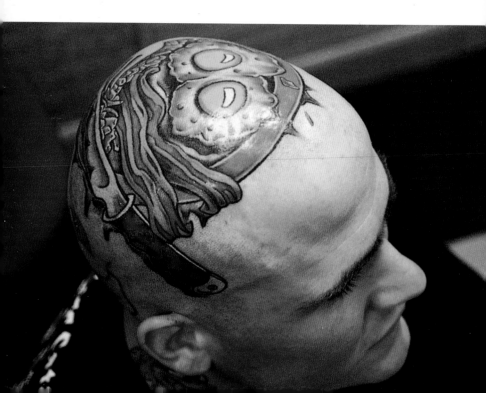

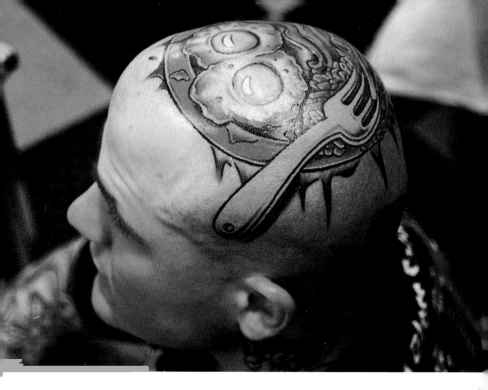

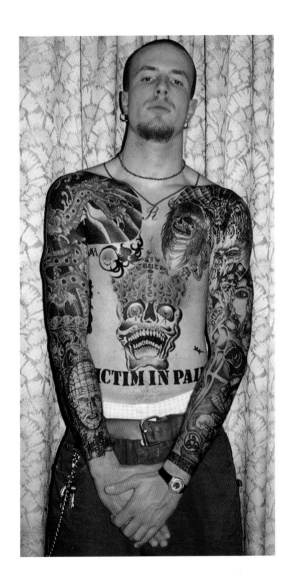

Tattoo: Tattoo Guus, Maastricht, The Netherlands

Tattoo: Filip Leu, Lausanne, Switzerland

Tattoos: Filip Leu, Lausanne, Switzerland

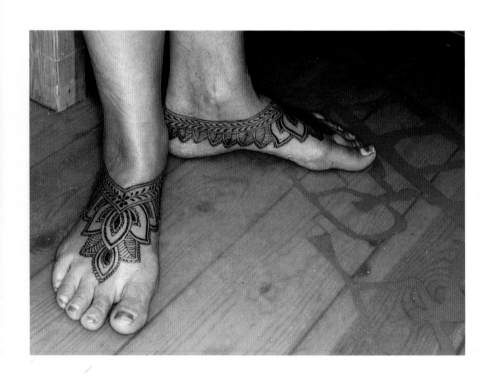

Tattoo: Erik Reime, Copenhagen, Denmark

Tattoos: Joel Dodds, Sacramento, USA (California)

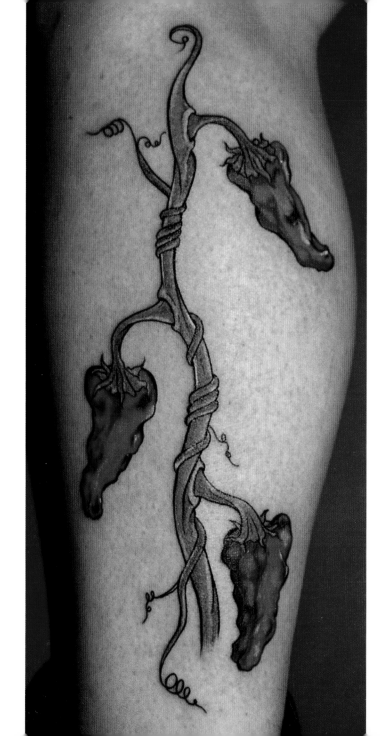

Tattoos: Eric Maaske, Fullerton, USA (California)

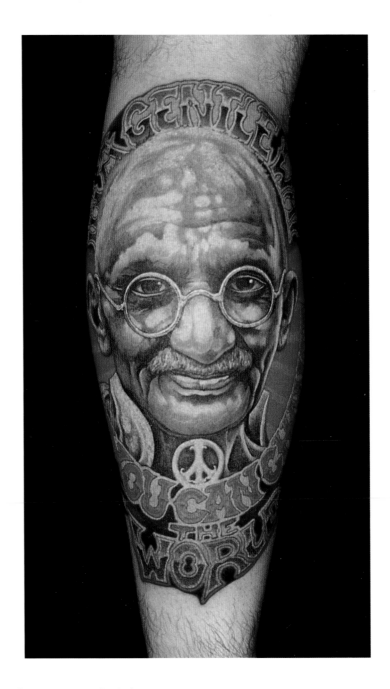

Tattoos: Filip Leu, Lausanne, Switzerland

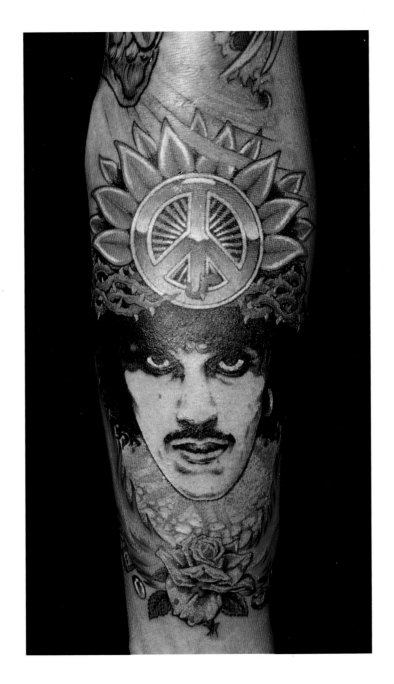

Tattoo: Felix Leu, Lausanne, Switzerland

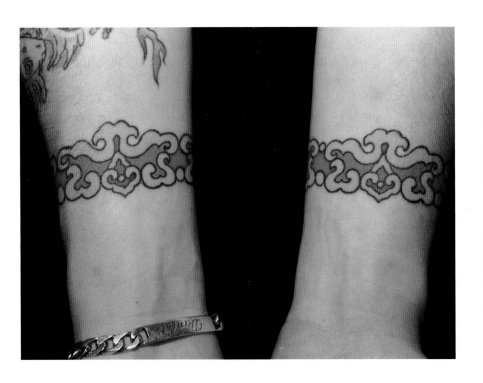

Tattoo: Felix Leu, Lausanne, Switzerland

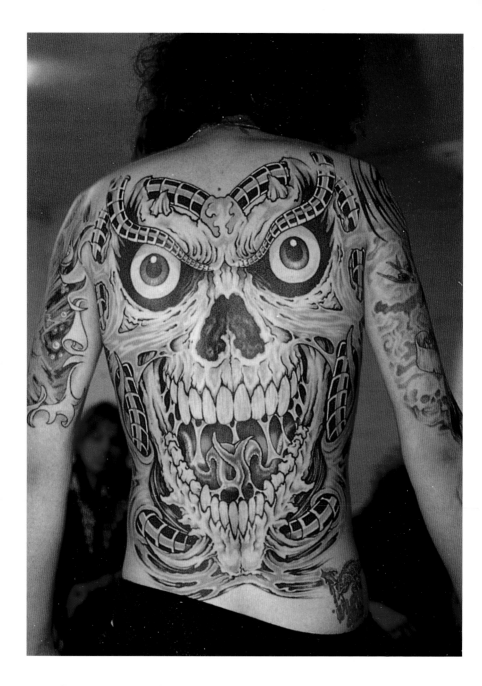

Tattoo: Filip Leu, Lausanne, Switzerland

Tattoo: Dave Shore, Vancouver, Canada

Tattoos: Horiwaka

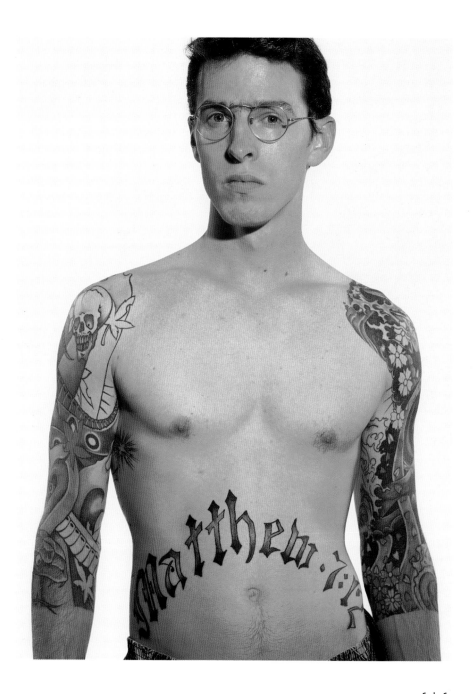

Tattoo: Lyon King, Portland, USA (Oregon)

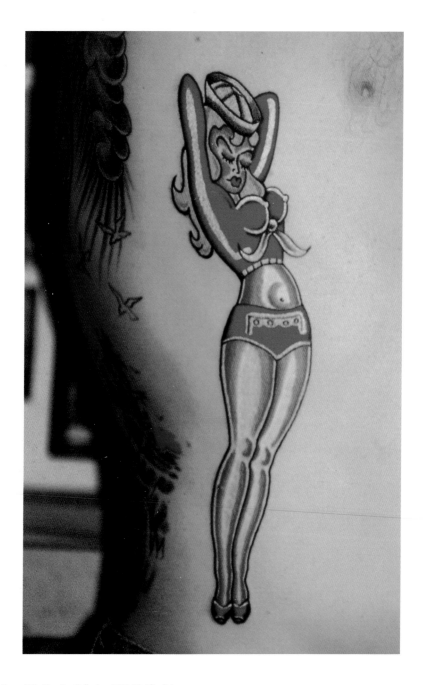

Tattoos: Eric Maaske, Fullerton, USA (California)

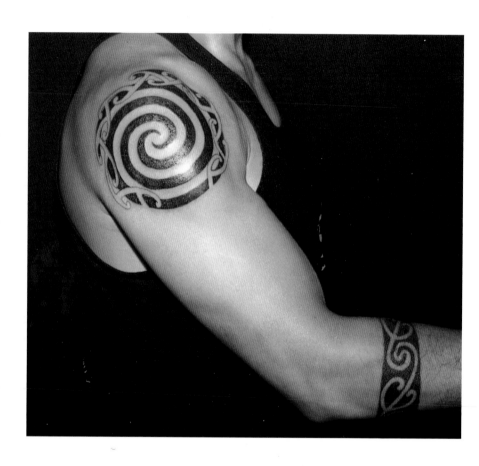

Tattoos: Roger Ingerton, Wellington, New Zealand

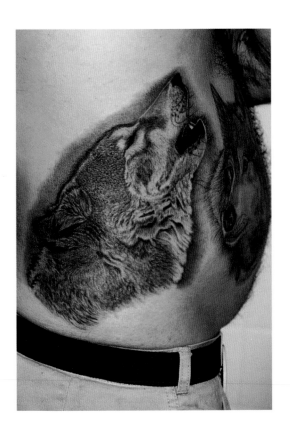

Tattoos: Brian Everett, Albuquerque, USA (New Mexico)

Tattoo: Jack Rudy, Anaheim, USA (California)

Tattoo: Marcus Pacheco, San Francisco, USA (California)

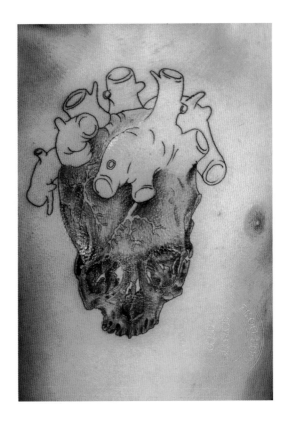

Tattoo: George Bone, London, Great Britain

Barber Unknown

Tattoos: Filip Leu, Lausanne, Switzerland

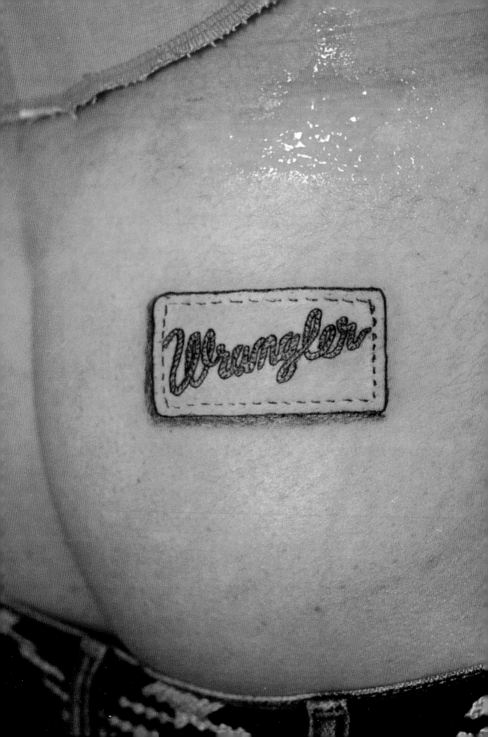

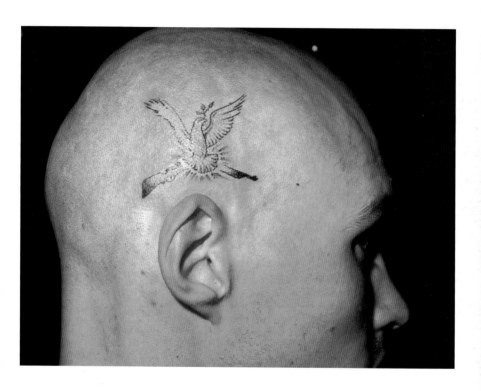

Artist Unknown

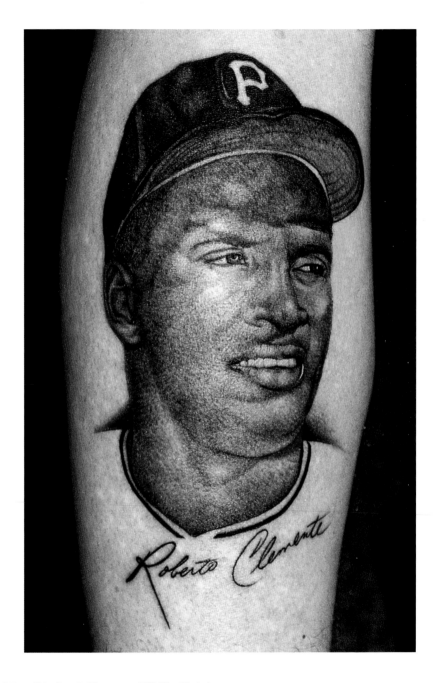

Tattoos: Brian Everett, Albuquerque, USA (New Mexico)

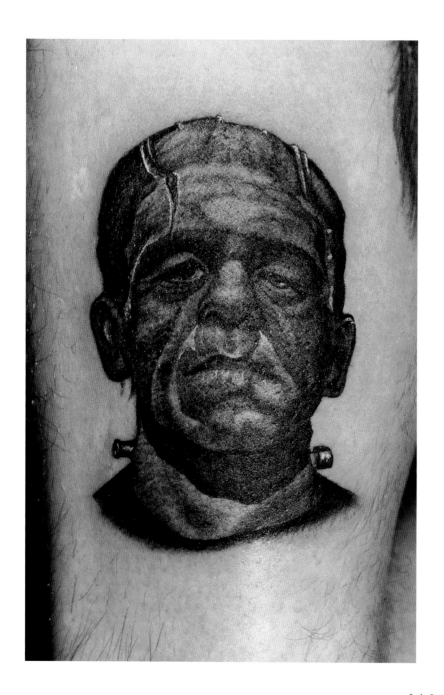

Tattoos: Luke Atkinson, Stuttgart, Germany

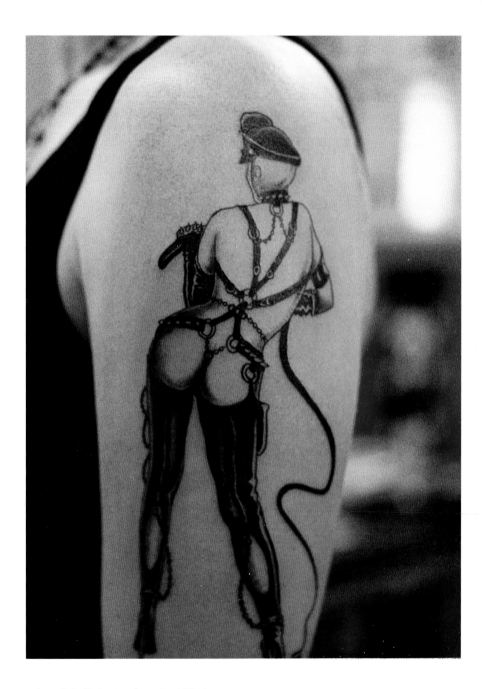

Artist: Nala Smith, San Francisco, USA (California)

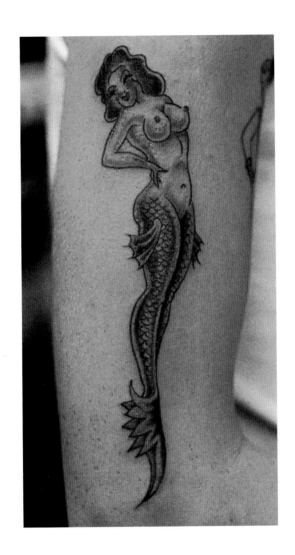

Tattoos: Henning Jørgensen, Helsingør, Denmark

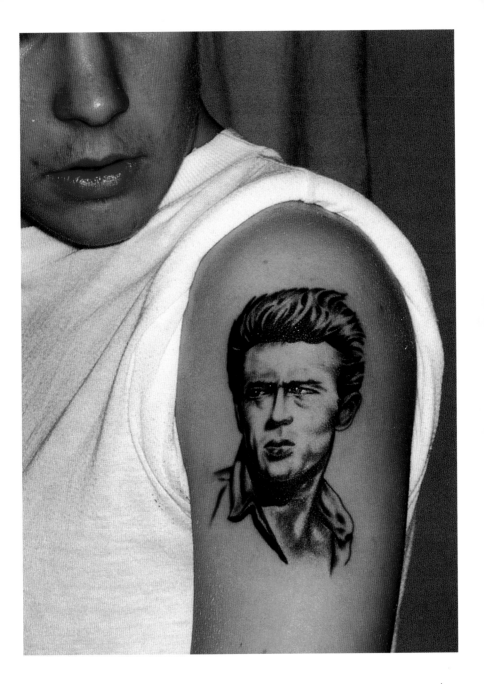

Artist Unknown

Tattoo: Martin Robson, San Diego, USA (California)

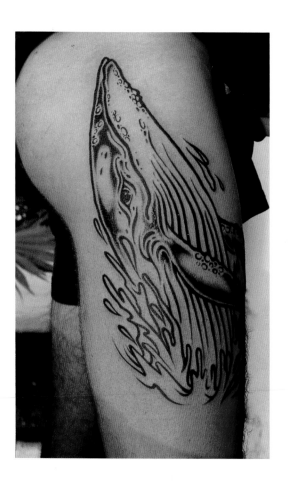

Tattoo: Henk Schiffmacher, Amsterdam, The Netherlands

Tattoo: Lance McLain, Wahiawa, USA (Hawaii)

Tattoo:s Tux's Tattoo Studio, Glen Burnie, USA (Maryland)

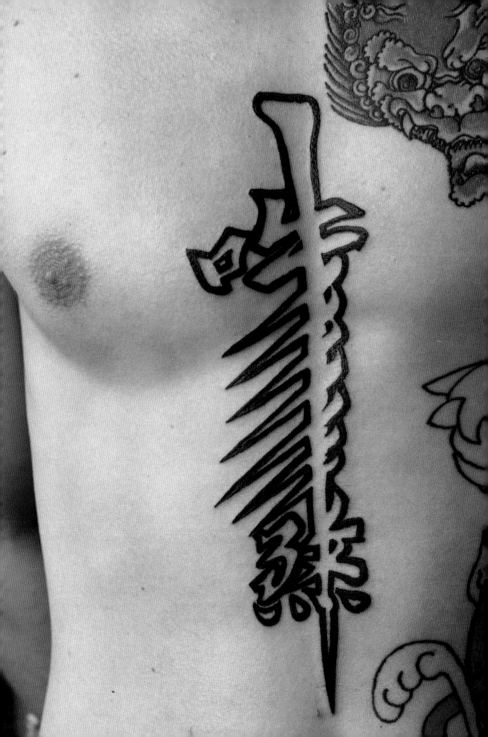

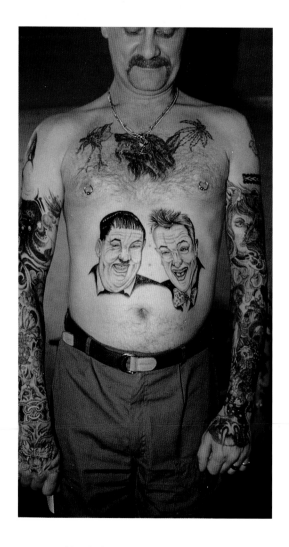

Tattoo: Ronald Bonkerk, Zaandam, The Netherlands

Tattoo: Jack Rudy, Anaheim, USA (California)

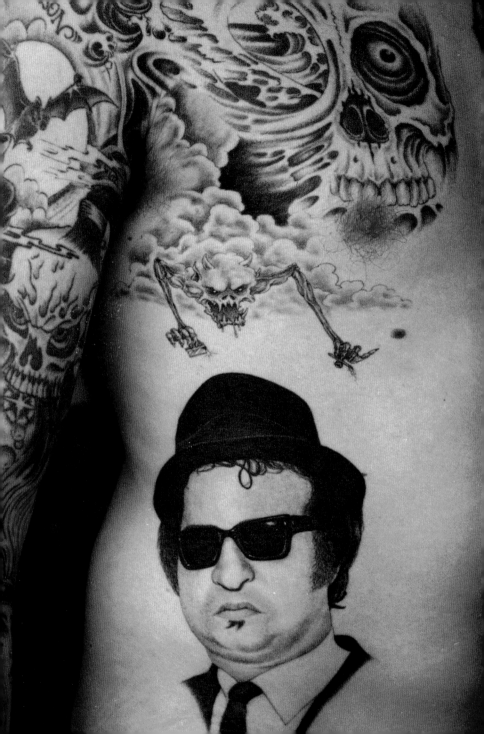

Tattoos: Fred Corbin, San Francisco, USA (California)

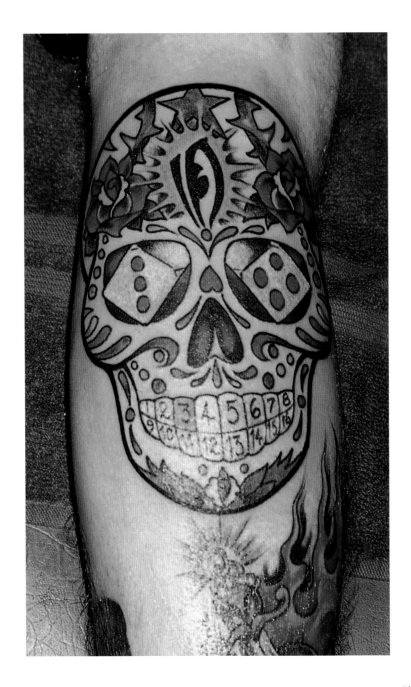

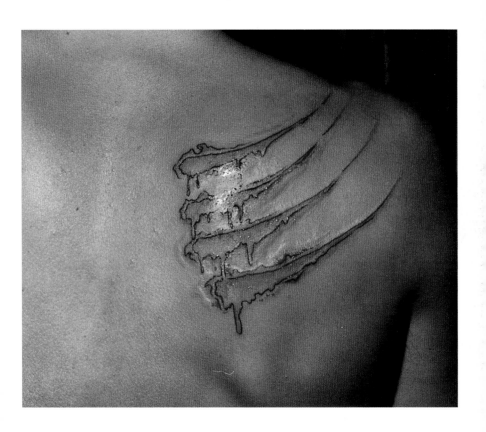

Artist Unknown

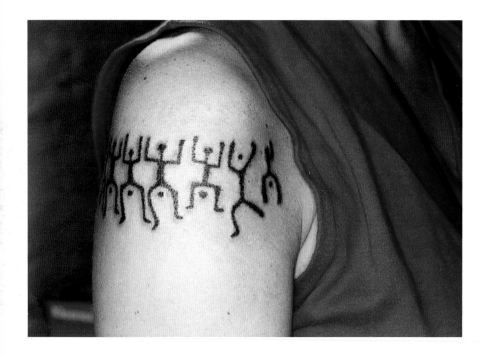

Tattoo: Erik Reime, Copenhagen, Denmark

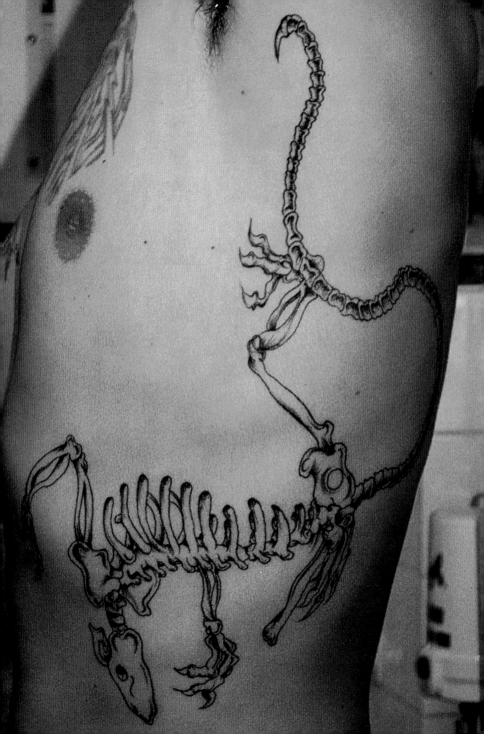

Henk Schiffmacher Tattooing Mark Almond
Photos: Patricia Steur, Amsterdam, The Netherlands

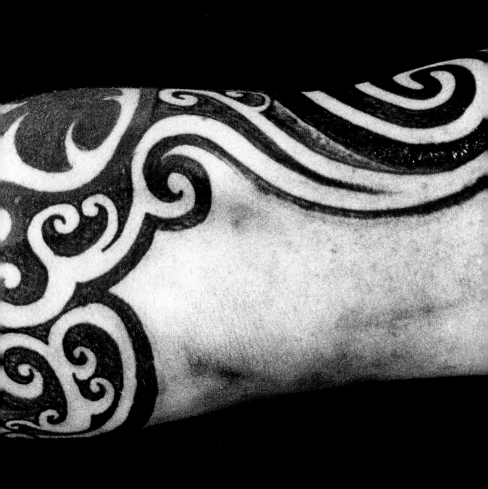

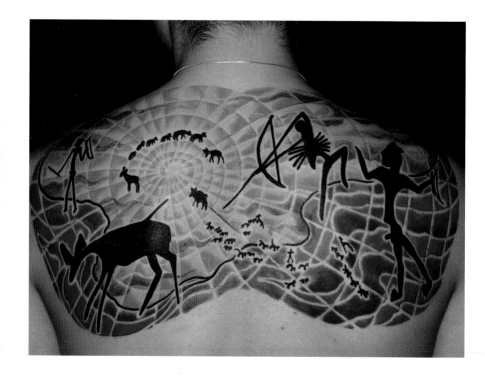

Tattoo: Luke Atkinson, Stuttgart, Germany

Tattoos: Brian Everett, Albuquerque, USA (New Mexico)

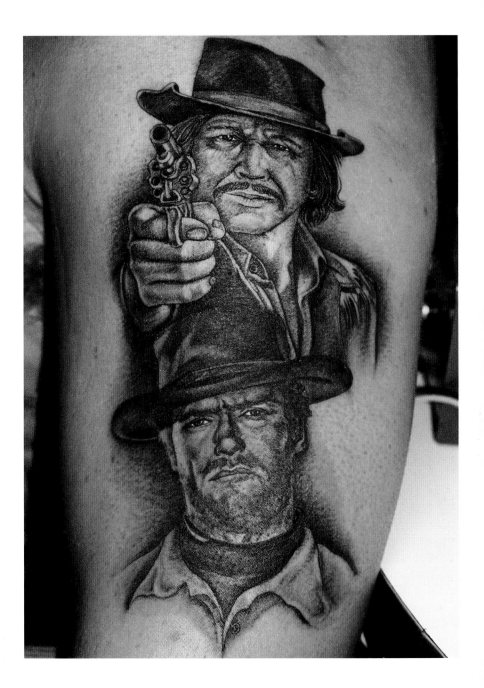

Tattoo: Suzanne Fauser, Ann Arbor, USA (Michigan)

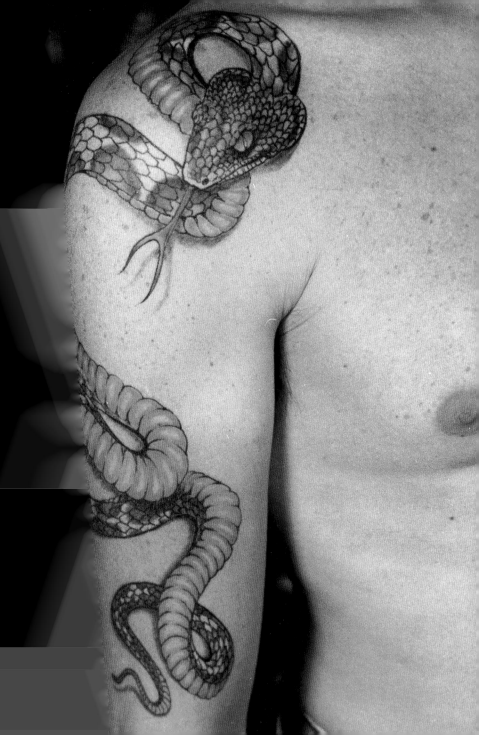

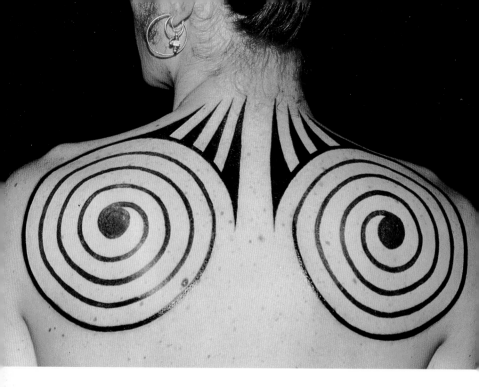

Tattoos: Roger Ingerton, Wellington, New Zealand

Tattoo: Marcus Pacheco, San Francisco, USA (California)

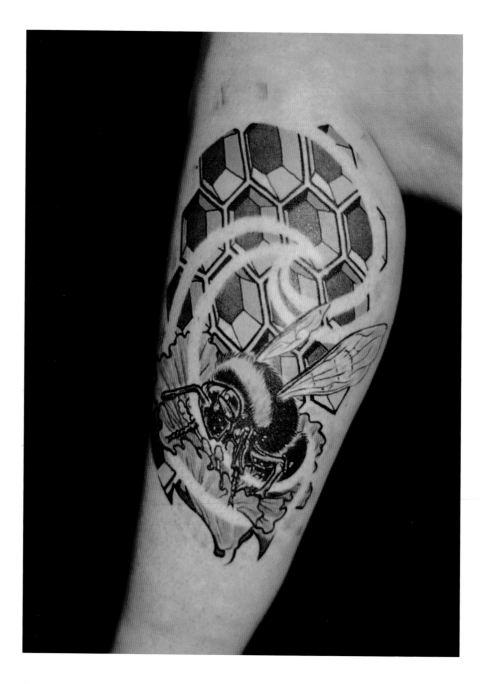

Tattoos: Marcus Pacheco, San Francisco, USA (California)

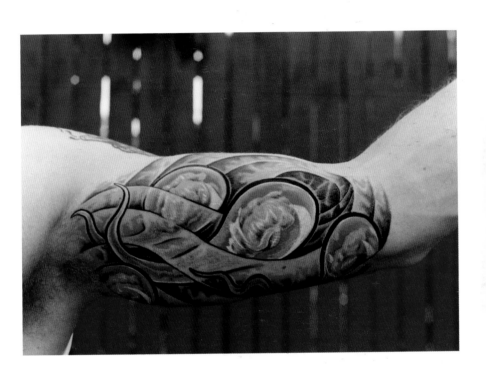

Tattoo: Tin Tin, Paris, France

Tattoos: Eric Maaske, Fullerton, USA (California)

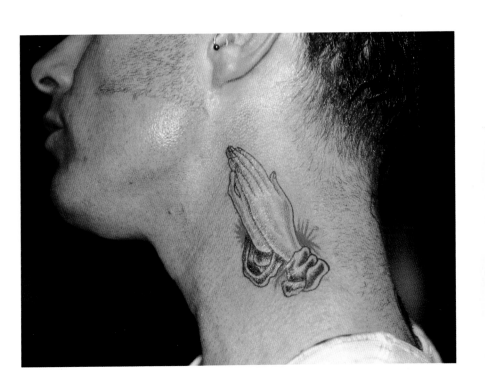

Tattoo: Alex Binnie, London, Great Britain

Tattoo: Andreas "Curly" Moore, London, Great Britain

Tattoo: Dave Lum, Salem, USA (Oregon)

Tattoos: Greg Ordi, Eindhoven, The Netherlands

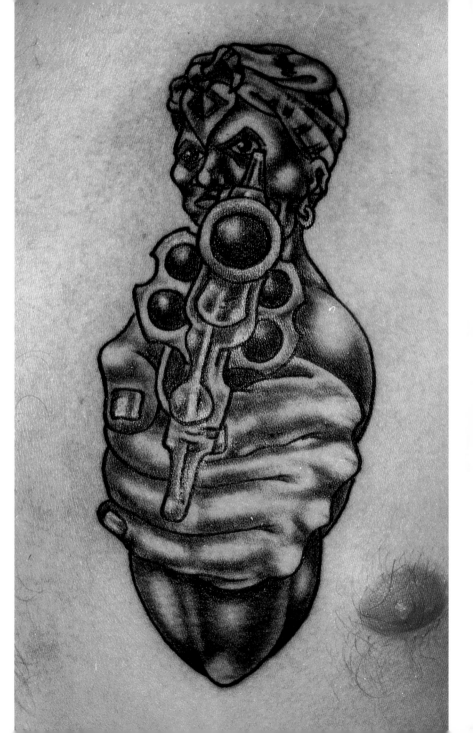

Tattoo: Marcus Pacheco, San Francisco, USA (California)

Tattoo: Eric Hogan, Sacramento, USA (California)

Tattoo: Luke Atkinson, Stuttgart, Germany

Tattoo: Greg Ordi, Eindhoven, The Netherlands

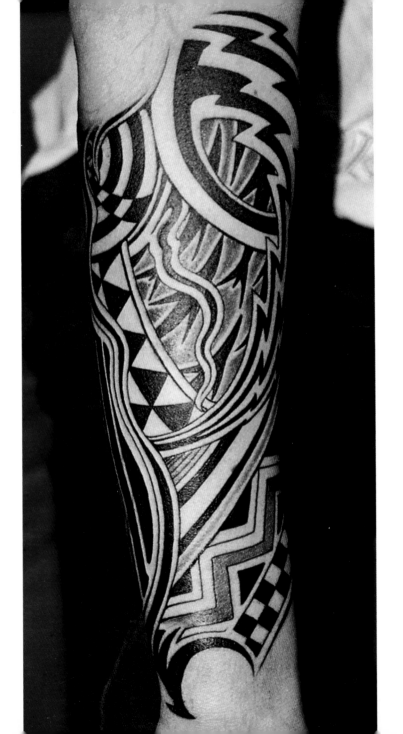

Tattoo: Eric Maaske, Fullerton, USA (California)

Tattoo: Dave Lum, Salem, USA (Oregon)

Tattoo: Alex Binnie, London, Great Britain

Artist Unknown

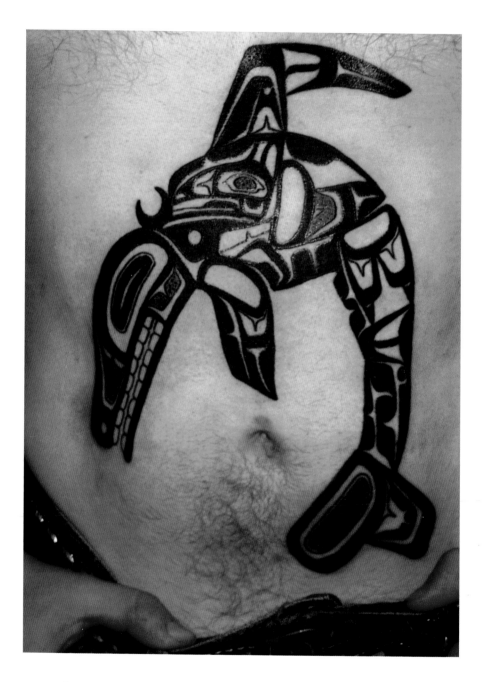

Tattoo: Andreas "Curly" Moore, London, Great Britain

Tattoo: Alex Binnie, London, Great Britain

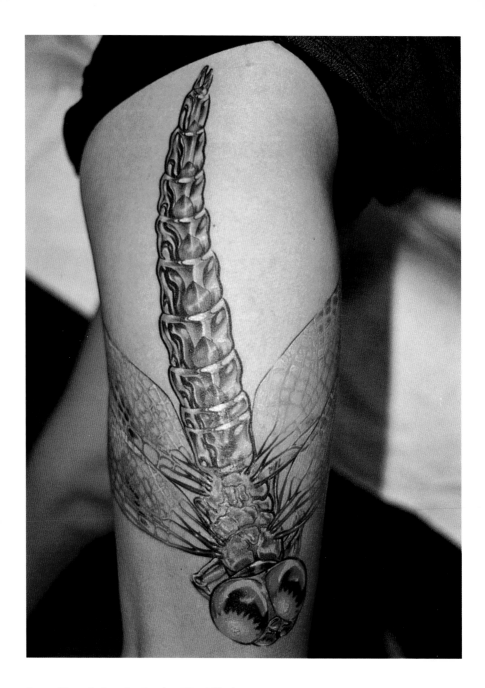

Tattoos: Marcus Pacheco, San Francisco, USA (California)

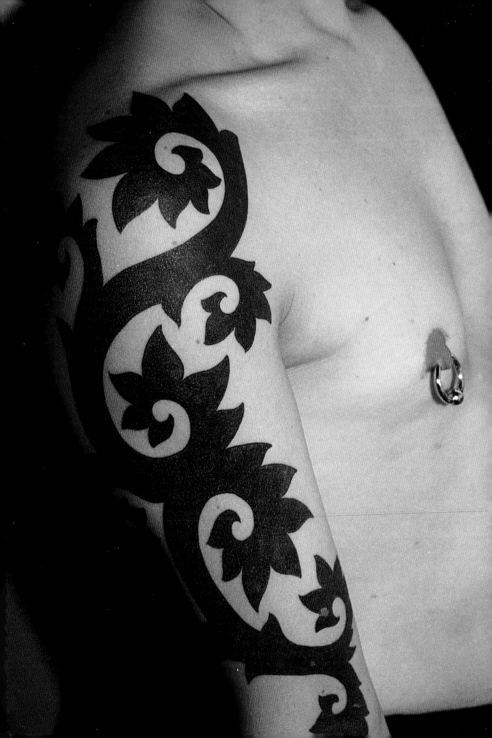

Tattoo: Andreas "Curly" Moore, London, Great Britain

Tattoos: Fred Corbin, San Francisco, USA (California)

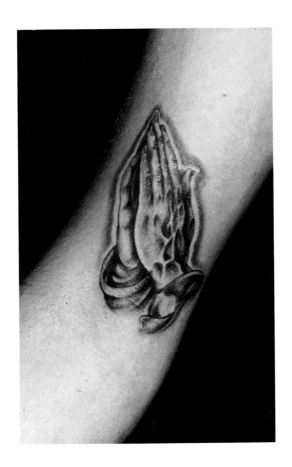

Tattoo: Scott Sylvia, San Francisco, USA (California)

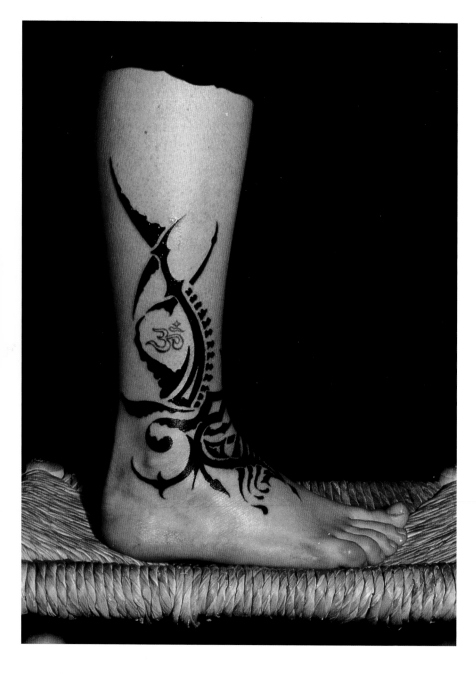

Tattoos: Filip Leu, Lausanne, Switzerland

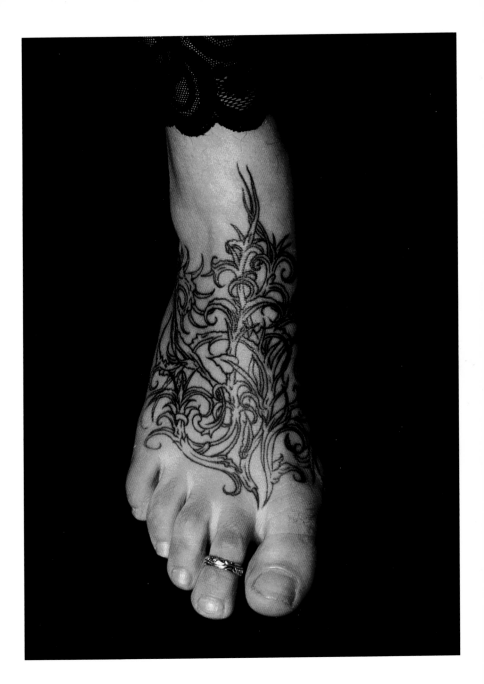

Tattoos: Filip Leu, Lausanne, Switzerland

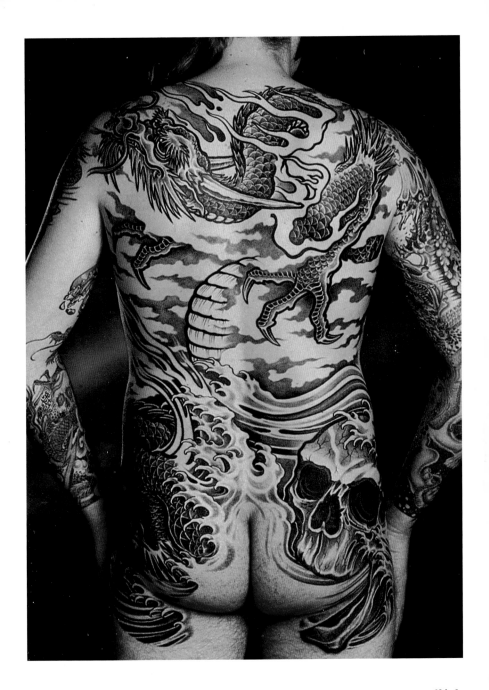

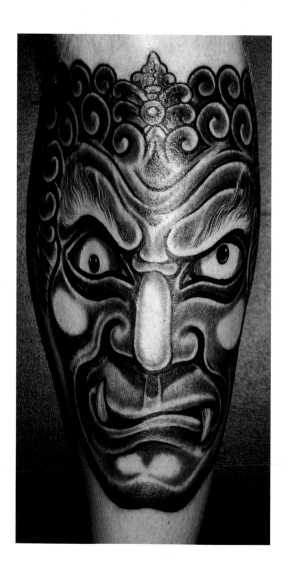

Tattoos: Filip Leu, Lausanne, Switzerland

Tattoos: Roger Ingerton, Wellington, New Zealand

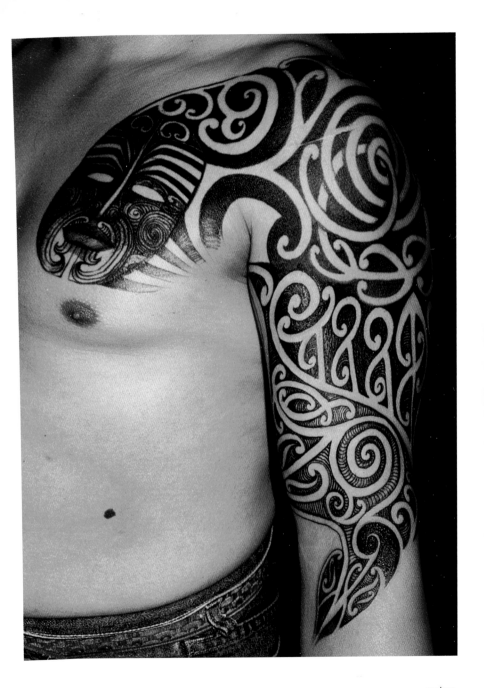

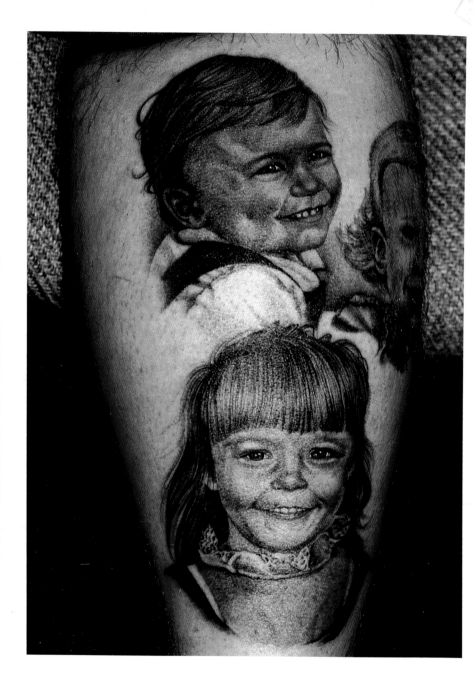

Tattoos: Brian Everett, Albuquerque, USA (New Mexico)